D1569084

THE REFORM OF EUROPE

THE REFORM
OF EUROPE

A Political Guide to the Future

Michel Aglietta

Translated by Gregory Elliott

VERSO
London • New York

330.94
A269

This work was published with the help of the French
Ministry of Culture – Centre national du livre
Ouvrage publié avec le concours du Ministère français
chargé de la culture – Centre national du livre

Cet ouvrage publié dans le cadre du programme d'aide à la publication
bénéficie du soutien du Ministère des Affaires Etrangères et du Service
Culturel de l'Ambassade de France représenté aux Etats-Unis.
This work received support from the French Ministry of Foreign
Affairs and the Cultural Services of the French Embassy in the
United States through their publishing assistance program.

First published in English by Verso 2018
First published as *Europe: Sortir de la crise et inventer l'avenir*

© Michalon Éditeur 2014
Translation © Gregory Elliott 2018

1 3 5 7 9 10 8 6 4 2

Verso
UK: 6 Meard Street, London W1F 0EG
US: 20 Jay Street, Suite 1010, Brooklyn, NY 11201
versobooks.com

Verso is the imprint of New Left Books

ISBN-13: 978-1-78663-254-8
ISBN-13: 978-1-78663-257-9 (US EBK)
ISBN-13: 978-1-78663-256-2 (UK EBK)

British Library Cataloguing in Publication Data
A catalogue record for this book is available from the British Library

Library of Congress Cataloging-in-Publication Data
A catalog record for this book is available from the Library of Congress

Typeset in Minion Pro by Hewer Text UK Ltd, Edinburgh
Printed and bound by CPI Group (UK) Ltd, Croydon, CR0 4YY

This work develops, and explores in greater depth, a number of themes broached in *Zone euro: éclatement ou fédération*, published by Éditions Michalon in 2012 in the midst of the crisis. A distance of two years has made it possible to undertake a more precise analysis of our persistent woes and to put the reforms required to escape them in perspective. An afterword updates the problems and perspectives to the end of 2017.

Finalization of this book has benefited from the criticisms and suggestions of Benoît Mojon (Banque de France) and Thomas Brand (CEPII), as well as a careful reading and formatting by Richard Robert (Paris Inovation Review). I am grateful to them. Any remaining errors are my responsibility.

Michel Aglietta

Contents

Introduction

At the time *Reform of Europe* was written – summer 2014 – the eurozone remained a source of concern. On average, the per capita GDP of member-states has still not returned to its level of late 2007. As for productive investment, it has fallen almost continuously, and is now roughly 20 per cent below its pre-crisis level. This deplorable situation affords an arresting contrast with the United States. It experienced a deeper recession than Europe following the peak of the financial crisis. But it was able to bounce back and comfortably outstrip pre-crisis levels of activity thanks to a revival of productivity at rates approximating to the past, when definitive losses due to the crisis are excluded. By contrast, the total productivity of all factors of production has fallen in Europe since 2007. There is no doubting that our continent is the sick man of the world economy.

Is this attributable to the inevitable decline of the 'old world' in the face of new, rising forces? Or to generally ageing populations, to a formal democracy that has run out of steam and is incapable of mobilizing citizens, to a social model not adapted to changes in the world? Or, more prosaically, is it the pusillanimity of Europe's political leaders, inheritors of a worthy project who lack the calibre to give it new momentum? Probably a bit of each. At all events, that is what I shall be endeavouring to find out here.

In a previous work, written in autumn 2011 and published by the same house,[1] I have already explored these issues. The crisis of the eurozone was at its height, and the question I raised was stark: break-up or federation? The financial crisis of 2007–08 did not spare Europe. Its banks were heavily involved in the international lobby whose excesses and malfeasance caused the crisis. But the key thing is that this shock exposed much deeper, much older structural flaws, which largely account for Europe's inability to drag itself out of stagnation. The affliction can be encapsulated in a phrase: incompletion of the euro. In effect, the euro is not merely the currency of the zone whose name it bears. It has become the basis of the whole European project. For the euro is intimately linked to financial unification, or the single market in financial services. The withdrawal of a sizeable country from the euro or, still worse, its disappearance would inevitably lead to capital controls, as indicated by the Cypriot example, and hence a regression in the European project.

In the crucial days of November–December 2011, when the European Central Bank had just changed presidents, the question was clear: Would the political leaders of the member-states have the convictions and lucidity required to save the euro? The answer was forthcoming in the first half of 2012. Two major decisions were taken: the signing of a treaty of fiscal union in March and plans to establish a banking union in June. These were significant events, because they indicated that member-states identified the euro as a common good which is the basis of the whole European project. It must therefore be defended at any cost.

Two years on, however, we find that these decisions, albeit central, have yet to improve either the effectiveness of political governance in the eurozone or the performance of its economies, which have sunk deeper into crisis. We need to understand what is happening. That is why the time was right for this new book.

It seeks to answer ten questions – questions which citizens concerned about their own future or that of their children are asking or might ask. Chapters 1 and 2 analyse what has happened since 2010: the crisis specific to the eurozone. We shall see how and why Europe ended up facing the threat of long-term stagnation. We shall also explore the institutional changes consequent upon the decisions of 2012, and see why they have not changed the governance of the eurozone, which remains paralyzed by disputes, suspicion and fragile compromises. The worst thing is the fiscal goals that governments and the European Commission persist in proclaiming, when they know them to be unrealistic: they are incompatible with fiscal consolidation in the wake of a financial crisis, and are not underpinned by a policy of shared growth.

Chapter 3 extends this general analysis, demonstrating that the heterogeneity of the eurozone's member-states is a handicap. The creation of the euro did not advance their cooperation in macroeconomic policy or lead to common political decision-making bodies. That is why the euro is an incomplete currency. As a result, monetary union has yielded the opposite of what its promoters hoped for. They anticipated a convergence in member-states' productive structures thanks to financial unification, which would finance productive investment in the new monetary zone's less advanced countries. In the event, what transpired was growing divergence: far from sustaining an upgrading of the productive apparatus, interest-rate convergence fuelled speculative property investment. After the financial crisis, this divergence brought about a polarization between creditor and debtor countries that has exacerbated political conflicts, deferred urgent decisions and converted them into half-measures. Persistent sharp policy conflicts between Germany on one side, and France and Italy on the other, over how to emerge from the stagnation sapping the eurozone while improving the public finances of all states remain a major threat. Germany's economic situation is less robust than it seems. The danger is a coarsening of political debate, leading throughout Europe to the pursuit of restrictive policies whose social consequences could increase the influence of populist movements in France and elsewhere, resulting in a dramatic decline of the European Community.

Chapter 4 focuses on France. Why is our country slowly but surely losing its productive capacity? A mistaken diagnosis blames the problem on the labour market, wrongly singling out especially high labour costs. This one-sided view ignores the responsibility of the increase in property prices since 1995 and in prices for corporate services, the shortage of innovative investment over many years, the poor social climate, and corporate governance dominated by financial control that encourages abandonment of home territory. Although advised of the fact, the Gallois report being an eloquent example of a wake-up call on the many reasons for the erosion of industrial competitiveness, the government decided to fix on a single cause – and not one peculiar to France: the widening gap in wage costs with

Germany. The authorities introduced the Competitiveness and Employment Tax Credit (CICE), without targeting firms that have competitiveness problems, and the responsibility pact, which is essentially a reduction in wage costs through the reduction of salaries. Nothing has been done about the key factors in the erosion of competitiveness – namely, a lack of investment and insufficient innovation by French enterprises.

Chapter 5 initiates a series of prospective analyses. Chapters 5–7 concern the eurozone's political governance. Can plausible strategies be identified to unblock the paralyzing governance that prevents completion of the euro? The thorny issues involved are dealt with in three chapters. Chapter 5 broaches reconstruction of a financial system capable of ensuring financial stability and providing long-term finance. This entails full implementation of banking union, but also expansion of the Central Bank's remit and allocation of a much greater role to non-bank investors in creating new instruments of corporate finance by establishing a public European investment fund. Chapter 6 deals with the strategy of fiscal consolidation. The lessons of historical experience allow us to define sustainable government debt rigorously, and to show that it is bound up with growth and monetary policy. These theoretico-political considerations lead on to the most decisive question for the euro's completion, which is the subject of Chapter 7: Is it possible to make the transition from a fiscal pseudo-union, characterized by a straightjacket of rules lacking credibility, to a system of cooperative action on member-states' fiscal policies, by pursuing the institutional process initiated by the 2012 treaty? It is possible to identify a progressive

approach involving institutional changes based on the existing European order, resulting, in the medium term, in an
integrated fiscal policy for the eurozone.

But a politico-institutional approach is insufficient. It is
also, and above all, necessary to give the European project
new meaning. Europe must recover what made for its specificity after the Second World War, if it wants to redeem the
soul it lost in financialization from the 1980s onwards. It
offered the most advanced model of social progress in the
world. Faced with the global challenges of the twenty-first
century, the goal must be inclusive, sustainable growth.
Chapter 8 demonstrates that in order to limit, and then
reduce, the forms of discrimination that fragment societies,
a new social contract is indispensable, whose foundation
lies in enterprises. The knowledge economy that is the
source of innovation requires enormous investment in
skills, involving close collaboration between enterprises
and public authorities in attacking all forms of discrimination that stifle productivity gains, not the least of which is
gender discrimination. These skills must be combined with
corporate strategies by instituting partnership governance.
The type of shareholding compatible with such governance
favours responsible institutional investors.

Chapter 9 endeavours to show that sustainable growth is
growth that makes the ecological transition a pole of attraction for innovative investment, in a growth regime capable
of rescuing Europe from stagnation. Current setbacks in
the German energy transition prove that its indispensable
basis is a common energy policy. The expediency of innovative investment in low-carbon technologies warrants reflec-
tion: here a finance scheme for public–private collaboration

will be proposed, aimed at overcoming the obstacles of double jeopardy, technological and ecological, which impede the development of such investment.

Chapter 10 concludes the book by showing that, if Europe pursues these objectives for a model of sustainable development, it can recover a political autonomy that will give it a mediating role in climate negotiations. Furthermore, if the eurozone's member-states succeed in equipping themselves with institutions of common governance, the euro can acquire the status of a fully fledged international currency. Europe could then find a monetary voice in international bodies. International monetary relations would become more polycentric – something that would require co-ordinated monetary governance. By merging their voting rights in the International Monetary Fund, the countries of the eurozone would align their external monetary policy with the existence of a complete euro currency, and would take a step towards the requisite reform of the IMF. In the areas of climate and monetary policy, Europe can play a useful role in producing general public goods for a non-confrontational form of regulation of the world economy.

1.

What Form Has Economic Policy Taken since the Greek Crisis?

As of summer 2014, the eurozone remained a source of concern, so patent was the political inability to restore vigour to its economies and hope to disillusioned public opinion. Much as happened throughout the West, the countries of the eurozone experienced the damaging effects of global financial crisis from the last quarter of 2007. But its relapse into recession in the second half of 2011 was peculiar to it, leaving it very weak. In 2014, its per capita GDP was about 2 per cent below its level of late 2007, reflecting absolute average impoverishment more than six years after the onset of the crisis. Not since 1945 had Europe suffered such a breakdown in growth. Yet government officials and Brussels bureaucrats have tirelessly repeated for years that everything will turn out all right, that recovery is already here, just as US President Hoover claimed in 1930–31. Manifestly, the eurozone has not found its Franklin Roosevelt.

The eurozone is the fulcrum of Europe. Were it to sink into protracted stagnation, which may be defined as the persistence of growth below 1.5 per cent, making it impossible to reduce unemployment, pursuit of the European project would become very difficult.

France's situation in the eurozone is particularly disturbing. Although household consumption maintained a comparative resistance to the crisis for a long time in France, the economy began a downward slide in 2012. The most significant indicator is the change in the average purchasing power of the income of the total population. Whereas it had grown at a rate of 1.8 per cent per annum between 2001 and 2011, it fell to –0.4 per cent in 2012, and only recovered very partially in 2013 (to 0.6 per cent), before stagnating on average in the first half of 2014. This stalling extended far beyond the 2012 recession. The slow decline in wages and inflation on the one hand, and the inexorable rise in structural unemployment on the other, are symptoms of a much more profound, much more enduring malaise. Whereas the average increase in nominal wages tended to be 2.4 per cent per annum in the years 2000–13, 2012 once again marked a decline: 2.1 per cent, followed by 1.7 per cent in 2013. This was accompanied by a deceleration in underlying inflation. From an average of 1.4 per cent since 2000 – already well below the 2 per cent norm – underlying inflation (which excludes volatile items vulnerable to price fluctuations) fell to 0.6 per cent in 2013, and then to 0.3 per cent in the first half of 2014.

Pronounced deflation would be not a problem, but a sign of good health, if it derived from a strong economy where productivity gains more than compensated for rising wage costs. But such is not the case. For labour productivity, which plummeted in the global recession of 2009 and bounced back strongly in 2010, slowed thereafter, and stopped increasing in 2013. Average productivity was back to its 2007 level – reflecting, in other words, a 0 per cent rise in six years. The unemployment pattern confirmed other economic indicators, pointing to exhaustion of the mainsprings of growth. The unemployment rate, which rose rapidly in 2012, was over 11 per cent in the eurozone, and remained above 10 per cent in France from the start of 2014.

To appreciate the significance of these disastrous developments, we must first assess the divergence between the evolution of the eurozone and that of other developed countries, especially the United States. This divergence involves the major macroeconomic variables, but also the mass of government debt and private debt and their variations in the crisis. We must then examine the major mistakes in economic policy largely responsible for these effects. Finally, we must begin to reflect on the impact that persistence in past and present errors might have on our future.

The United States and the Eurozone: The Great Divergence

Figure 1.1 depicts the comparative development of three key macroeconomic variables: real GDP, real investment and real credit, all measured per capita.

Developments in GDP and investment leave no room for doubt. The United States and the eurozone experienced the financial crisis consequent upon the collapse of the US property market and that of several European countries, and the shock wave it set off in finance, in similar fashion. The development of GDP was closely correlated until September 2011. It then diverged until a worldwide business cycle started in 2017. Meanwhile, the United States posted a recovery, while the eurozone was plunged back into recession.

Figure 1.1: Comparative Developments
in the USA and the Eurozone
1a: Per Capita GDP

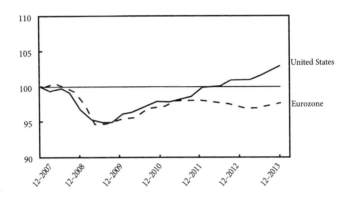

1.1b: Per Capita Real Investment

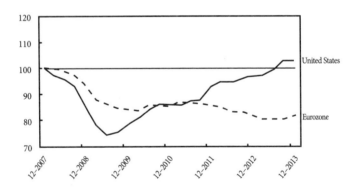

The profiles are much more sharply contrasted when it comes to per capita investment. In the United States, it fell 25 per cent between the onset of the recession in December 2007 and the nadir of September 2009. It then recovered and progressed continuously, in December 2013 reaching a

1.1c: Per Capita Real Credit

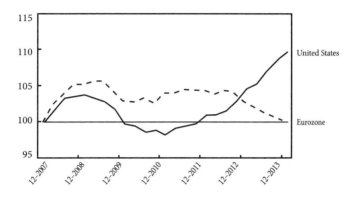

Source: Fed and Eurostat, in Natacha Valla, Thomas Brand
and Sébastien Doisy, 'A New Architecture for Public
Investment in Europe', *CEPII Policy Brief*, no. 4, July 2014.

level 3 per cent above that of December 2007. This 3 per
cent increase over six years (approximately 0.5 per cent a
year) brings home the persistent impact of the crisis. It
shattered the pre-crisis trend growth rate (what is called
potential growth). But that is as nothing compared with the
effects of the dual crisis experienced by the eurozone. At the
outset, it held up better, since the initial low point, in March
2010, represented a fall of 16 per cent since December 2007.
But the recovery was slow up to March 2011 (3.9 per cent).
And thereafter investment fell back sharply. Overall, in
December 2013 it was 18 per cent below its December 2007
level! At the same point in time, the zone's GDP was still 2
per cent below its 2007 level. When investment declines
over such a long period, it produces attrition of the stock of
productive capital, with (as we shall see) a series of negative
consequences for growth factors.

For now, however, we may note that these disturbing developments are not independent of finance. An initial, very general indicator of credit is the flow of per capita real credit, which comprises lending to households and enterprises. What does it reveal? First of all, lending in the eurozone withstood the downturn occasioned by the peak of the financial crisis in September 2008 better than in the United States, where an extended credit squeeze occurred. From December 2008 to December 2010, per capita credit in the non-financial private sector fell by 5.4 per cent. It then recovered uninterruptedly, in December 2013 reaching a level 10 per cent above December 2007. In the eurozone, by contrast, per capita private credit was still 4 per cent higher in December 2010 than in December 2007, and it fell back to that level in December 2013. Thus, we observe no expansion in per capita real credit in six years!

These developments represent a significant break with rates of lending prior to the financial crisis. This does not mean that all was well beforehand. Credit expansion was excessive in numerous countries, which experienced inflation in property prices and transactions.[1] The upshot was over-indebtedness of households and enterprises, which proved unsustainable when the value of the assets supposedly guaranteeing debts collapsed. The need for debt reduction was the primary cause of the recession, followed by difficulties in restoring private sector expenditure (household consumption and corporate investment). As we shall see, the United States and Europe diverged in their treatment of the after-effects of the financial crisis.

Private debt and government debt in the financial cycle

In the OECD countries, the debt burden on the real economy increased continuously during the quarter-century preceding the financial crisis of 2007–08. On average, every year saw a 1.15 per cent increase in the debt of (public and private) non-financial agents, to finance a 1 per cent rise in nominal GDP. Because debt servicing is consuming a growing share of national income, such financial rent cannot increase indefinitely.

Because the rise in the debt to GDP ratio is not permanent, the debt–growth interaction operates in two directions. An increase in debt stimulates growth, but a high level of debt depresses growth, because it dictates debt reduction. The change of phases – from growing indebtedness to debt reduction – passes through a bifurcation point called a financial crisis. The sequence of phases leading up to the return of indebtedness, once the losses from the crisis have been settled, constitutes a financial cycle.[2] The massive transformation of finance prompted by deregulation and globalization from the 1980s onwards has intensified the financial cycle. Increased indebtedness leads to growth in domestic demand, and then an overvaluation of asset prices, abrupt changes in which expose over-indebtedness. This prompts a reduction in demand and triggers recession, and then the slow and difficult debt reduction that stabilizes balance sheets. The duration and periodicity of financial cycles (fifteen to twenty years) are significantly greater than those of conjunctural GDP cycles (five to eight years).

In a financial cycle, recession may be longer and deeper than in a 'normal' business cycle. It is followed by a phase of stagnation because the restoration of conditions for growth requires, in the first instance, the absorption of financial losses and consolidation of borrowers' and lenders' balance sheets. This is what is called balance-sheet deflation.

The financial cycle is always generated by private debt. Why, then, are European governments obsessed by public debt? It is because government debt ballooned to save the banks when the crisis became systemic, when states injected money into the economy to prevent recession turning into a depressive spiral. In short, states are borrowers of last resort when private agents cut their expenditure simultaneously. That is why government indebtedness is counter-cyclical. To offset the effects of private debt reduction, a policy of fiscal expansion must be pursued. This is hampered if government debt levels are already too high prior to the downturn in the financial cycle.

As we can see, the problem is not the level of government debt per se, but the ability of the public sector to cushion the depressive consequences of private sector indebtedness. Here, when studying the interdependence between private debt and government debt, we observe a twofold contrast between the Anglo-American countries and the eurozone, on the one hand, and between the major countries of the eurozone themselves, on the other (Table 1.1).

Let us relate the results of Table 1.1 to the developments in Figure 1.1. Private debt fell substantially in Britain and America because growth restarted there, thanks to expansionary fiscal policies in particular. Logically, the burden of government debt therefore increased. The Japanese anomaly stems from a

Table 1.1: Government Debt and Private Debt
2013 level and 2008–13 variation as a percentage of GDP
1.1a: Eurozone in the OECD

	2013 Level		2008-13 Variation	
	Non-financial private sector debt (households and enterprises)	Gross government debt	Non-financial private sector debt (households and enterprises)	Gross government debt
United States	156	85	- 19	+ 22
Eurozone	164	96	0	+ 26
Britain	187	89	- 16	+ 34
Japan	167	238	- 3	+ 46

Source: National accounts, AMECO data base, Groupama-AM

1.1b: National Debt in the Eurozone

	2013 Level		Variation 2008-2013 (%)	
	Non-financial private sector debt (households and enterprises)	Gross government debt	Non-financial private sector debt (households and enterprises)	Gross government debt
Germany	107	80	- 7	+ 13
France	123	92	+ 13	+ 24
Italy	128	127	+ 6	+ 21
Spain	209	94	- 11	+ 54

Source: National accounts, AMECO data base, Groupama-AM

combination of the repercussions of the current financial crisis and the unresolved crisis experienced in the early 1990s. Japan is a classic example of a country where debt was already very high in 2008. At this level of debt, counter-cyclical effectiveness is very low: government debt grew significantly for a modest reduction in private debt. As to the eurozone, government debt rose without any fall in private debt. To understand what happened, let us compare variations in private debt with cumulative growth over the same period (Table 1.2).

Table 1.2: Growth and Development of
Private Debt 2008–13 (percentage)

	Cumulative growth	Variation in non-financial private sector debt
Germany	+ 3,0	- 7
France	+ 0,5	+ 13
Italy	- 8,4	+ 6
Spain	- 7,4	- 11
Eurozone	- 2,1	0

Source: same as Table 1

The eurozone presents a highly variegated picture. Thanks to growth, albeit modest, Germany was able to reduce the private debt burden through a limited expansion of government debt. In Spain, private debt had reached absurd levels with the explosion of the real estate sector. Its collapse automatically reduced private debt at the cost of a severe, prolonged recession, leading to a surge in government debt. The Spanish 'adjustment', widely derided, has left a scene of devastation: 25 per cent unemployment, 50 per cent youth unemployment, a haemorrhage of human capital pocketed by Germany for free. Italy is the paradigm case of a eurozone economy approximating to Japan. An already very high pre-crisis level of government debt has paralyzed counter-cyclical policy. Seeking to pursue an austerity policy, the country has inflicted a prolonged recession on itself, which has seen a rise in the burden of government and private debt alike. France is the paradigm case of a country that has ended up stagnating, and where, as a result, all debt is increasing inexorably.

The question that arises is thus the following: How is it that countries linked by monetary union have proved so incapable of cooperating to manage the financial cycle?

The Cardinal Errors of Economic Policy in the Eurozone

The global financial crisis reached its peak in September–October 2008. At the time, cooperation worked. Central banks took charge of the international liquidity market, which was completely frozen by the inability of commercial banks to renew their cross-borrowing. The G20 decided on a concerted fiscal stimulus, which was very sizeable in the United States and China. Interest rates in the money markets rapidly fell to levels approaching zero in the United States and the UK. In November 2008, these countries' central banks embarked on the initial phase of a policy of quantitative easing by buying utterly worthless mortgage securities[3] and government debt securities. To make it clear that liquidity would remain plentiful, the two central banks announced that interest rates would stay in the vicinity of zero long after the economies emerged from recession. Above all, from February 2009 the US Federal Reserve undertook an audit of the state of bank balance sheets to identify the scale of unrealized losses, followed by a stress test to assess the capital injection required to stabilize the banks' financial situation. In April 2009, an unconditional recapitalization out of public funds to the tune of $700 billion was carried out. The result can be found in Figure 1.1c on p. 13. Six months later, the collapse of credit in the private sector was halted and, in the course of 2010, it started to recover.

The crisis was therefore met with a closely coordinated expansionary fiscal policy and an ultra-loose monetary policy, with the pledge that it would persist for several years, and a banking policy of consolidation committing very considerable public funds. What happened in Europe in the same period? A mixture of conservative economic doctrine, completely ill-suited to the so-called 'liquidity trap' in which all private actors are reluctant to spend, an inability or disinclination to clean up balance sheets, and extraordinary paralysis in the face of the Greek state's insolvency – these factors created the split between the eurozone and the rest of the world. It is not that nothing was done. But it was invariably too little, too late.

The overly timorous stabilization of bank balance sheets

In a financial crisis that brought an end to years of excessive lending – excess motivated by a massive bubble in asset prices, not by anticipation of a tendential increase in income from economic activity – losses on assets were enormous. Many borrowers have net negative wealth because the value of their debts is now greater than that of their holdings. They are unable to repay their loans. Their insolvency impacts on banks. If the latter do not wish to acknowledge their bad loans, they artificially renew their debtors' credit. If the authorities do not force banks to acknowledge their losses – something true of the German authorities in particular

– balance sheets become unreliable. This means that many economic agents – banks prominent among them – report positive profits when they are in fact negative. But the reality is reflected at a macroeconomic level. What is called the 'natural' interest rate – the nominal equilibrium interest rate of an economy achieving its growth potential, without inflationary pressures or unemployment above its structural level[4] – becomes negative.[5] The central bank can reduce the market interest rate at most to the zero-rate barrier.[6] The economy therefore cannot bounce back fully. It accumulates spare productive capacity. This leads to protracted stagnation, as we shall see in the third section of this chapter.

We can now understand the close link that must exist between an ultra-loose monetary policy and the bank policy of stabilizing balance sheets. The role of the former is to ensure that market interest rates remain very low after the onset of recovery, so as to encourage new investment, absorb spare productive capacity, and make it possible to replace obsolete capacity. The latter raises the natural rate after having identified and absorbed losses. For the natural rate must be persistently higher than the market rate in order for strong growth to be self-sustaining and for unemployment to fall.[7]

In Europe, the European Central Bank (ECB) only seriously initiated an 'unconventional' policy from 2010, and then in dribs and drabs, because it was fettered by its statute, laid down in the Maastricht Treaty, which prevented it from purchasing government securities, and by German hostility to any unorthodox measures. An orthodox policy in a far from orthodox context was incongruous. The ECB fully performed its role of lender of last resort from the onset of the crisis. But for a long time it sought to separate this role from monetary policy, which was too tight in the circumstances because the ECB's reluctance to lower its base rate pushed the market rate above a natural rate highly influenced by losses attributable to the crisis. Nevertheless, as we shall see in Chapter 2, it bought covered bonds and government securities from countries subject to aid programmes (Greece, Portugal and Ireland).

But the role of governments was much more harmful. The banks were dependent on national regulatory authorities much more inclined to maintain existing arrangements than to stabilize balance sheets. Each national authority was jealous of its prerogatives, whereas the banks were enmeshed in interlocking commitments throughout Europe via their networks of branches and subsidiaries. They were therefore trans-national. But it was not until June 2012 that the indispensability of a banking union, if the euro was to survive, was recognized; and the results of the assessment of bank balance sheets prior to the requisite recapitalization only became known in late 2014 – five-and-a-half years later than in the United States.

The inability to prevent the spread of the Greek crisis

It was the Greek crisis – the crisis of a country that accounts for no more than 5 per cent of eurozone GDP – that plunged it back into protracted recession. Its diffusion via the banks was rapid. For the Greek state and banks were insolvent at the same time, in a vicious circle in which each of the partners dragged the other down. Greek banks are an integral part of the eurozone's inter-banking system. Other

Mediterranean countries affected by the global crisis (Spain and Portugal), or suffering from very high levels of government debt and already weak banks (Italy), were trapped in a spiral of worsening government debt and deterioration in the condition of banks holding government securities. The Anglo-American mutual funds that held these countries' government securities, and which were also large depositors, withdrew abruptly, causing a hike in rates on government debt and thereby reducing its value in Spain, Italy and Portugal – something that led to a further sharp deterioration in bank balance sheets.

What did governments do to stop this race into the abyss? They did everything to deny that the Greek sovereign debt crisis was a solvency crisis. For as long as possible, they treated it as a temporary liquidity crisis. To the contrary, a partial default plan to contain the sovereign debt crisis should have been arranged at once. This could have been done by the reconversion of existing debts into long-term bonds with lower interest rates and the joint guarantee of the eurozone governments. But national governments and the ECB needed to accept the loss of their claims on Greece in order to arrive at an adequate reduction of the government debt, which would have made it possible to reflate the country's economy. Candid early acceptance of a default would have substantially loosened Greece's financial constraints and enabled it to return to the road to growth, instead of which Greece suffered a depression, losing 19.5 per cent of GDP between mid 2008 and the end of 2013. Could things have been handled worse?

The policy course followed by the European Council and Commission was so short-sighted that successive rescue plans had to be concocted to keep Greece in the eurozone: an initial €109 billion in summer 2010, followed by €110 billion in summer 2011, as against €37 billion contributed by private creditors via a 50 per cent haircut on the Greek securities they held. The net result of the so-called rescue was therefore a massive transfer from private creditors to the eurozone's taxpayers. It also increased Greek indebtedness, when what an insolvent country needs above all else is debt reduction. Obviously, the main private creditors are the eurozone's banks, either directly or indirectly through their claims on Greek banks. The banking lobby's ability to dictate to governments at the expense of any democratic rules attained its zenith here. The fragmentation of political power in Europe in the face of a unified banking lobby largely explains the public authorities' inability to take a firm stand in negotiations with private creditors.

The Abrupt Switch in Fiscal Policy:
From Joint Reflation to Simultaneous Austerity

It might be said that this is tantamount to a gross error of macroeconomics motivated by ideology. No doubt it was bound up with a sense of panic over the Greek crisis. The German government regarded Greece as the epitome of the irresponsible policies it suspected among all its partners in Southern Europe. The crisis therefore had be overcome by expiation on the part of the guilty, who had to reform themselves to restore their competitiveness. The problem is that this moralizing attitude, while certainly in accordance with the European Commission's economic ideology, was incompatible with economic rationality in the context of a financial cycle marked by the private sector's need to reduce its indebtedness. Let us take a closer look at this crucial issue.

The slogan that justified the switch in fiscal policy was as follows: Austerity and growth! To the layperson, the idea that stronger growth can be achieved by reducing government expenditure might seem aberrant. But it is not impossible. Let us take the case of a small country located in an external economic environment that it may regard as stable, because the country is too small for its economic policy to have an impact on the rest of the world. As a result of conflicts over distribution, a new government comes to power with the mission of cutting public expenditure, because it has promised to increase private wealth creation more rapidly. It is not necessarily sheer demagogy if a reduction in the state's economic weight alters the conditions in which private actors take their decisions.

In the case to hand, reduced public expenditure means less government borrowing in the capital markets, and hence lower interest rates on government bonds. The central bank can extend this dynamic to the whole economy by lowering its base rate. The cost of capital is thereby reduced, which may induce firms to invest. They are all the more likely to do so if the fall in domestic interest rates depreciates the national currency's exchange rate and thereby improves the competitiveness of domestic firms, expanding their market share. In addition, if it is genuinely believed that economic rationality extends to decisions about the future, and if the government is credible, households will anticipate a reduction in taxes in the future. This should lead them to reduce their saving and consume in the here and now. In short, it is possible for the ratio *variation in GDP/fiscal stimulus*, known as the multiplier, to be negative, and for GDP to increase through a fall in public expenditure. At the very least, if GDP falls, it will do so less than the downward momentum of fiscal expenditure. The multiplier is said to be lower than one. The shock of austerity is absorbed.

This case is interesting not only because it furnishes arguments for austerity policies, but above all because the underlying hypotheses are the precise opposite of the eurozone's situation in the overall financial cycle. National governments and the Commission could not have been unaware of this. They are therefore responsible for a deliberate increase in unemployment on the pretext of rapid consolidation of government debt. The result can be seen in Tables 1.1b and 1.2 (p. 18): GDP fell, unemployment surged, and government debt, rather than being reduced, escalated. If Germany emerged unscathed, it is because it was able to avoid recession thanks to its ability to export to the rest of the world, itself the fruit of old comparative advantages.

To show that this was bound to be the case, let us take the hypotheses of the scenario analysed above one by one. I referred to a small country that implemented an austerity policy singlehandedly. In the case of the eurozone, we are not dealing with austerity in one country, but in several countries simultaneously. The eurozone comprises a group of countries amounting to a very sizeable economy, which has an impact on the rest of the world. This means that a general austerity policy in the eurozone reduces global growth, and hence Europe's exports to the rest of the world.

The recessionary shock was therefore terrible. It occurred in the worst possible conditions, because the world economy had not recovered from the financial crisis, unemployment in the eurozone was already very high, and private actors were desperately trying to reduce their debts when the recessionary fiscal shock supervened from late 2010. There was therefore no chance of private household demand taking over from public expenditure, even if future taxes were regarded as bound to be lower – which is doubtful. The financial pressures experienced by households prevented this kind of juggling between current and future expenditure.

As to the other offsetting mechanism – a fall in interest rates – it was impossible, because they were already at zero. Inflation therefore began to fall with demand still weak, and already considerable idle surplus productive capacity.[8] Consequently, real interest rates rose, rather than falling, and the euro appreciated in value rather than depreciating. The result was empirically predictable. The multiplier *variation in GDP/variation in fiscal stimulus* was superior to one – in fact, of the order of 1.5. It was the greater because all eurozone states made budgetary cuts at the same time. With a negative fiscal stimulus of 1 per cent, GDP fell by 1.5 per cent. This was enough to plunge the eurozone back into recession for two years.

The multiplier was higher because the expenditure sacrificed was predominantly public investment – the expenditure that has the most traction in the economy. Figure 1.2 shows, furthermore, that the attrition of public investment in the Eurozone is not a recent development. Its decline is a long-term phenomenon. As a percentage of

Figure 1.2: Public Investment in the Eurozone
Percentage of GDP

Source: Fed, Eurostat, Paredes *et al.* (2009), Giannone *et al.* (2012)

GDP, it has fallen in stages since the start of the 1980s. We should note the impact of the economic stimulus plan from autumn 2008, which led to a recovery in investment expenditure until autumn 2009, and then the sharp drop over more than three years until the first quarter of 2013.

The key issue is the long-term consequences of this policy. I will have occasion to explore the effects on the structural weaknesses of the eurozone in Chapters 3 and 4. Let us conclude the present chapter with a macroeconomic investigation of growth potential.

The Trap of Secular Stagnation

Secular stagnation is defined as a persistent dip in the growth potential of an economy to a rate that is insufficient to reduce structural unemployment to a level compatible with financing the basic public goods on which social stability depends. In France, given demographic dynamics, this minimal long-term growth is of the order of 1.3–1.5 per cent per annum on average. It is not compatible with the policies that have been pursued over the years 2009–14. The cumulative growth of the eurozone between 2008 and 2013 was −2 percent, and that of France +0.5 per cent. To restore potential growth of 1.3 per cent, a short-term acceleration would be required far in excess of this trend rate, between 1.8 per cent and 2 per cent over several years. Such dynamism appeared only in 2017. Growth for 2014 was predicted to be 0.4 per cent, and 1 per cent in 2015.

The hypothesis of secular stagnation extends beyond the eurozone. The issue haunted the annual research conference staged by the IMF in November 2013.[9] The clarifications presented here make it possible to formulate it. This can be done if we reject the dominant assumption of neoclassical growth theory. It postulates that long-term supply is independent of demand. It follows a trend that depends solely on demography and technological progress, which is supposed to be exogenous, like manna from heaven. For its part, finance, in this conception of the economy, has no influence on long-term growth. In this theory, technology is regarded as a *deus ex machina*, independent of all charac- teristics concerning views on the future expressed by finance (Figure 1.3).

The historical data collected by international organizations – first and foremost, the Bank for International Settlements (BIS) – demonstrate that this is not the case. The growth of credit and asset prices – i.e. estimates of capital profitability

Figure 1.3: Naïve Conception of the
Cycle and Long-Term Growth

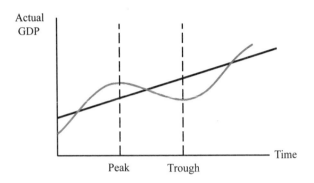

Potential GDP is independent of conjunctural fluctuations
and hence of demand. Actual GDP revolves around and
constitutes the business cycle.
Output gap = (Actual GDP-Potential GDP)/(Potential GDP)

– reveal long-term financial cycles. It follows that the
interaction between the financial cycle and trends in the
real economy is close.

In the descending phase of the financial cycle subsequent
to a crisis, weaknesses in the real economy are persistent.
The restoration of productivity is very slow and lowers the
long-run trend. Inflation is low, systematically below
monetary policy targets. Uncertainty about the quality of
financial assets checks innovation. The most effective
theoretical hypothesis for explaining such phenomena is
balance-sheet deflation. It prioritizes finance for the
purposes of understanding major long-term fluctuations
in growth. For the development of the financial cycle in its
expansionary phase is not an efficient process. It entails

over-indebtedness, over-valuation of assets leading to bad investments, distortions in the allocation of real resources, and the accumulation of weaknesses in finance itself. The interaction of these distortions accounts for the gravity of the financial crisis. It provokes balance-sheet recession – that is, the dangerous process of devaluation of over-valued assets and debt reduction. This logic imposes itself on the whole economy, impeding both demand and productivity gains. Figures 1.4a and 1.4b (p. 33) describe these sequences.

These figures refer to a completely different conception of growth from that captured in Figure 1.3. Total supply and demand interact on a long-term basis, since both depend on the estimates and options of finance, which condition corporate investment decisions and household juggling between saving and consumption. In the expansionary phase of the financial cycle, choices are swept up in the euphoria when everyone looks to profit from the rise in the prices of assets (such as property). Because the anticipated rise in asset prices increases the profit expected from acquiring assets, everyone has an interest in going into debt to purchase them. Lenders make the same calculations because the assets bought by their borrowers are also the collateral that guarantees loans. This self-reinforcing logic is called momentum. It creates speculative bubbles – that is, hikes in value that are imaginary in the sense that they cannot deliver the future income they promise. That is why every speculative bubble ends up bursting, at some unforeseeable point in the future. When this occurs, the financial crisis is triggered. The momentum is reversed and brings about a catastrophic fall in the asset prices that had been swept up in the bubble. Falls in asset values reverberate in losses on the loans that borrowers cannot repay – something passed on to the lenders. But the latter form a network of counterparties, such that some people's defaults are other people's losses. The rush into debt in the euphoric phase turns into a rush to debt reduction in the phase of stress and fear. But to reduce debt in an orderly fashion – that is, absorbing losses without one's activity being adversely affected – it must be possible to allocate sufficient income to provide for losses. This is impossible when a large number of people are seeking to reduce their debt, and therefore spend less. The transmission of financial constraint to the economy depresses private sector demand, so that debt reduction is counteracted. A protracted fall in growth ensues.

In the eurozone, this process – called balance-sheet deflation because it is the losses incurred in balance sheets that are the main cause of the lack of demand in the real economy – has been aggravated by policies of fiscal austerity initiated at the worst possible time. The vicious circle of protracted insufficiency of demand (Figure 1.4a) then contaminates supply (Figure 1.4b). When previous excesses polarize current options towards balance-sheet deflation, supply and demand interact and are pointed in the direction of protracted low growth. That is why macroeconomic policy in Europe is so ineffective. Expansionary fiscal policy only has a moderate impact, but austerity policy greatly exacerbates weak demand. Monetary policy faces enormous difficulty preventing a situation where unduly low inflation makes debt reduction more difficult, because real interest rates remain too high compared with the natural rate.

Figure 1.4: The Low Growth Trap
1.4a: The Demand Side

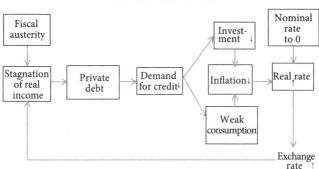

1.4b:The Supply Side

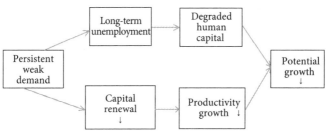

In the current European situation, repairing the balance sheets of financial intermediaries is therefore the priority if there is to be any hope of reviving credit. It involves the full, complete realization of banking union. The latter is indispensable if monetary policy is not to continue to be trapped by the banks' inability to do their job. To acknowledge losses, recapitalize, and enforce respect for the prudential rules that maintain provision of sufficient liquidity, to prevent overuse of debt leverage – these are so many preconditions for any willingness to reinvest.

But that is not all. We have seen that eurozone countries find themselves in different circumstances, while they form a unified monetary zone where countries' reciprocal influences upon one another are both intense and asymmetrical. To control this interaction in a way conducive to reconstructing a growth regime, what is required are strong institutions capable of promoting collective action by member-states. Here, too, the eurozone has serious obstacles to overcome.

2

What Institutional Initiatives Have Been Taken since the Crisis?

Europe is characterized by the inability of its countries to pursue effective policies in concert – and this in all areas. In Chapter 1, we saw how mediocre macroeconomic performance has been. The inability to cooperate affects foreign policy as well as energy and transport, social policy as well as minimal tax harmonization. We live in a common monetary area without a public sphere at the European level, and hence without institutions that could animate democratic life, providing a source of coordination and collective choices. That is why it is rightly said that the euro is an incomplete currency. It is shared by economic agents in market transactions, but it is foreign to states. This singular state of affairs derives from the ambiguous motives behind the euro's creation. It has persisted in and through the political logjams that have arisen over time. That is why the eurozone possessed neither the resources for joint action, nor – above all – the clear-sighted political leaders, let alone the democratic legitimacy, to assert the long-term interests of the European project when confronted with the devastating shock of the financial crisis.

Nevertheless, governments proclaimed their desire to maintain the eurozone's integrity in adversity. This is a gain of great significance. Had the interests of states been inherently contradictory, there would have been nothing to prevent the breakup of the eurozone or the withdrawal of some of its members. Why bother to remain in a union if one believes that the cost of exit is outweighed by the advantages to be derived from exit? The threat hanging over the eurozone is therefore not that of a crippling rivalry, but of a lack of coordination. Viewed from this angle, solutions to the problem exist not in a paradigm shift that would establish a political union in some foundational catharsis, but in a course of institutional development feeding off obstacles and perils to progress.

I am going to show that this dynamic has begun by describing the initiatives taken and endorsed since the Greek crisis in 2010 in the monetary, banking and fiscal spheres. On this basis, we may reflect on some proposals for pursuing institutional change to completion of the euro. First of all, though, we must understand what an incomplete currency is.

The Incompletion of the Euro

Let us start by clearly understanding what currency is. It is not a commodity, but a social contract. For it is the shared *medium* wherein, in the act of paying, the collectivity using it renders to each of its members what it reckons it has received from them in the form of activity. The payments system is therefore the public good that validates the social utility of everyone's activity. The currency governs the dynamic of debts that accounts for the cohesiveness of societies organized in accordance with a multitude of separate exchanges. To be able to settle debts, the currency itself has the nature of a debt. It is the ultimate debt acknowledged and accepted by all. It is defined as the debt of society as a whole to itself. It is therefore radically distinct from private debts. In this, currency is the quintessential common good.

We can now understand why currency is the most general social bond. It belongs to all those who accept it as an undoubted, unquestionable common good. In a world where human collectivities are organized as nations, it forms part of national sovereignty. If we clearly distinguish between the nominal source of power, which is popular sovereignty grounding legitimacy, and the real source of power, which is the monopoly on legitimate violence held by the state and validated by the constitutional order, shared trust in the currency partially escapes the state. This trust is ethical in kind, since it is based on awareness of a shared affiliation, represented by acceptance of the social medium that is currency. The state codifies the rules in accordance with which currency is issued, circulates and settles transactions. When these rules are assimilated by the currency's users and go unchallenged, trust in the state's authority – also called hierarchical trust – suffices to guarantee the monetary order. It follows that monetary crises, when the rules are rejected and, with them, the legal tender (in hyper-inflationary crises), are also crises of the state. Hierarchical trust is destroyed. To restore the monetary order, it is necessary to re-establish the sense of collective belonging, and hence the cement of ethical trust.[1] This idea is hard to understand in France, where revolutionary principles have identified popular sovereignty with the state. But it was inherent in German monetary union prior to the euro. The Deutschmark was introduced with the Basic Law before the Federal Republic was created, politically and chronologically preceding the creation of the federal state. The Central Bank's independence from the political executive is an institutional device to create distance between the maintenance of ethical trust in the currency and public policy.

The founding principle of Federal Germany is ordo-liberalism, which received legal expression in the Basic Law of 1948. The latter establishes the sovereignty of the people. It is above the state, because it formalizes society's most deeply embedded moral values in a constitutional order. The legal order is an obstacle to any arbitrary power, whether issuing from the state through a political majority or from coalitions of private agents (oligopolies, cartels, lobbies). However, vis-à-vis the economy, the state is far from being minimal, contrary to the ultra-liberal conception of Anglo-American observance. But its activity must respect the institutional framework of the market. The institutional framework is distinguished from market mechanisms: its keystone is the currency. Currency stability is much more than an objective of economic policy. It is a categorical imperative of the Basic Law. Currency stability is constitutive of the social order, over and above the political. That is why an independent institution must be responsible for it.

But its dimension as a social bond is only one aspect of currency. The other is the organic bond between currency and state via the social debt. This debt is distinguished from private debts in that it is the debt of every member of society to society as a whole. In effect, as a member of society, over the course of his or her life every individual disposes of public goods that account for the cohesiveness of societies: free or subsidized education, health services, security, infrastructure, urban cultural facilities, and so forth. The totality of real assets that make up these public goods, and which create public services, constitutes society's collective capital. This is the debt of every member of society to society as a collective power, whose organization is the precondition for individual existence. Every member of society consumes the services of the collective capital. This debt is honoured by the tax stream owed by adult individuals throughout their life. The legitimacy of taxation is the counterpart of recognition of the common good. Taxes are levied by the state as society's tutelary power. Government debt – the financial debt of the state (in the broad sense) – results from an intergenerational transfer, where the state decides to go into debt in order to create public goods, and hence to finance them by deferred taxes. This intergenerational transfer establishes the abiding cohesion of society. In effect, when the state invests in collective capital, it enhances the nation's capacity for future production, which increases future incomes. It follows that the future generations that will benefit from this increase in collective capital will be wealthier and will help repay the government debt through which the collective investment was financed. Since government debt is the temporal dimension of the social debt, and since the latter is the debt of individuals to society as a whole, government debt does not have the same status as private debts, even when held by private agents. In every country where the state is not a failed one, it must be possible to remove government debt from the vagaries of markets by guaranteeing its liquidity. This is a key task of the central bank. There follows an organic link between state and currency.

These two dimensions – the currency as bond of trust between citizens and the currency as the *medium* in which the social debt is honoured – account for the ambivalence of currency.[2] It is the constitutional order, guaranteeing both the bond of trust and the solvency of the social debt, which defines the completeness of the currency.

The euro is an incomplete currency because this constitutional order is absent

The ECB is the sole federal instance in a group of nations that are not united by any democratically established constitution. It is a currency that is not backed up by a social debt acknowledged in the same space. That is why the statute of the Central Bank in the intergovernmental Treaty of Maastricht prohibited it from buying the government debt of member-states. This rule, which is unique in the world, results from the contradictory character of the organization of European monetary union. The ECB issues a currency that is common to the citizens of the member countries, but foreign to the states. In the former dimension, the Eurozone is more than an international currency regime, because it has a central bank and a unified system of payments. But in the latter dimension, the euro is a foreign currency with fixed exchange rates for all states. In effect, the eurozone countries are deprived of the organic link, which exists everywhere else, between central bank and sovereign state. In any country that issues the currency in which government debt is denominated (hence if government debt is not issued in foreign currency), and where the state is not a failed one, government debt is sheltered from default, because the state has the ultimate capacity to monetize its debt and thus remove it from the market. This results from the reciprocity of the organic link between central bank and state. The state is the ultimate guarantor of the central bank's capital. The central bank is the lender of last resort in the financial system, whose pivot is government debt.

The financial crisis had devastating effects in the eurozone because this link did not exist. When the crisis exposed Greece's insolvency, panicked private creditors attacked the government debt of solvent states because, in accordance with the dictates of the Maastricht Treaty, the monetary authority was prevented from playing its role as lender of last resort. The treaty was thus bound to exacerbate national rivalries between creditor and debtor countries in conditions of financial crisis. In their turn, these rivalries have led irreversibly to the fragmentation of the European financial area, which the creation of the euro was intended to unify.

That is why the European Council of the heads of state and the ECB found themselves backed into a corner. In the absence of an organic link between currency and states, as a matter of the utmost urgency they had to offer ad hoc, substitute institutional responses, on a step-by-step basis punctuated by developments in the crisis. These expedients must be described, so as to discover whether they represent a move towards completion of the euro. These institutional innovations involve the monetary and banking sphere, on the one hand, and the fiscal sphere on the other.

Initiatives in the Monetary and Banking Sphere

The crisis began at the start of August 2007 with the inability of BNP Paribas to price certain monetary funds in dollars, whose yield was pushed up because they were invested in securities constructed out of sub-prime credits. By mid August, the whole inter-bank credit market had seized up. The central banks hesitated to supply the banks with liquidity. However, while the Anglo-American central banks began to reduce their key rates from autumn 2007, the ECB did not budge. In July, it even raised its rate out of a fear of inflation, following a spike in the prices of agricultural raw materials. It therefore confined itself to 'qualitative easing'. The composition of the assets in the Central Bank's balance sheet changed under the impact of last-resort lending operations. But its size remained compatible with a monetary policy ignoring the crisis, thanks to compensatory operations known as sterilization, which consist in the sale of securities to withdraw the additional liquidity injected by last-resort loans.

Events took a different turn in the United States after the collapse of Lehman Brothers in September 2008. Panic having been ignited like a powder trail, and having manifested itself in a general demand for ultimate liquidity by the private sector, the Fed and the Bank of England at once made the transition to 'quantitative easing'. The size of the Fed's balance sheet increased from $800 billion to $2.2 trillion in a few weeks in autumn 2008. With the cross-swap agreements (reciprocal loans) by central banks decided at the start of October 2008, the ECB's balance sheet likewise swelled, but by much less, from €650 billion to €1 trillion, roughly, €210 billion of which were procured by cross-currency swap agreements. But monetary policy remained very cautious, the ECB seeking to reduce the size of its balance sheet during 2009 thanks to emergence from recession half-way through the year. When the Greek crisis erupted, the size of its balance sheet had fallen back to around €800 million.

With the discovery of Greece's insolvency in May 2010, there began an era of initiatives that represented a series of violations of the Maastricht Treaty, which loftily ignored the very possibility of general financial crises, beyond the last-resort lending reserved for banks. Henceforth debates inside the ECB became more bitter. Pragmatism was now imperative, and the influence of Bundesbank dogmatism receded on the monetary policy committee. The ECB innovated in two ways: new forms of injection of liquidity into the economy, applied to the weak links of financial vulnerability that revealed themselves successively; and relaxation of the rules governing the collateral that the banks had to put up to obtain liquidity from the ECB.

Provision of liquidity and relaxation of collateral

From 14 May to 9 July 2010, the European Council had to resign itself to the ECB buying in the secondary market government securities of the three countries subject to the aid programmes of the troika (European Commission, IMF and ECB), in operations dubbed SMP (Securities Market

Programme). This was a timid foray into the technique of quantitative easing that was the spearhead of the Fed and the Bank of England. At the same time, the ECB resorted to a modest covered bond purchase programme from July 2010, to the tune of €60 billion. Added to this was an extension of operations providing liquidity to banks and a modification in technique. Refinancing operations became potentially unlimited in their amounts, at fixed price and for an extended duration. These are the famous long-term refinancing operations (LTRO) that enjoyed the ECB's support, because they were geared to the benefit of banks and therefore did not call its mandate into question. A modest programme was put in place in May 2010: €36 billion in six-month loans. The worsening of the financial situation in autumn 2011 led banks to withdraw to their home territory and threatened the whole eurozone with a credit freeze in November 2011. The ECB decided to launch an LTRO refinancing operation of unusual scale and duration. In two phases (December 2011 and February 2012), it proceeded to two re-financings over thirty-six months at a zero interest rate, to a cumulative amount of the order of €1 trillion. The size of its balance sheet reached €2.5 trillion. This operation, on a completely different scale from what had previously been undertaken, brought some respite on the financial markets. Interest rates on the government debt of weak countries ebbed, but lending to the private sector did not recover.

The other type of action to make banks' lives easier was relaxation of the rules of the collateral pledged by them to access ECB refinancing. On 3 May 2010, the minimum quality rating was abolished for Greek, Irish and Portuguese assets. From September 2011, the relaxation became much more significant: assets that were so risky as to be excluded from transactions on regulated markets were accepted by the ECB, but with a substantial haircut; and asset-backed securities were accepted. Finally, the rule of the homogeneity of collateral was abandoned in February 2012, allowing national central banks to set their own rules.

Interventions that were modestly described as 'unconventional' only temporarily stopped the panic in financial markets, and by no means halted the recession in the eurozone. On the contrary, the crisis was seriously exacerbated from August 2011, partly as a result of fiscal problems in the United States. The ECB had to switch scale without expanding the panoply of resources it had created. Hence the episode of the thirty-six month LTRO, which enjoyed only a qualified, short-term success in lowering long-term interest rates on government bonds in countries (Spain, Portugal and Italy) where government debt was under attack from speculators banking on a fall in its value, prompting the mass sale of these bonds by Anglo-American institutional investors. All efforts were unavailing, and in April–May 2012 the financial crisis broke out afresh.

June–September 2012: the crucial decisions and their repercussions

The lesson of these repeated failures is that the short-sighted crisis management imposed on the ECB by government procrastination treated only the symptoms, not the profound causes, of the disrepair of finance. Balance-sheet deflation continued to gnaw away at financial institutions insidiously, plunging economies into recession. Financial fragmentation had reached a point where the ECB alone was preserving the superficial unity of the eurozone. The inability of governments to restructure and recapitalize banks in the weak countries, and the reluctance of creditor countries to contribute to the process directly, threatened the euro's existence.

It was now, at the dramatic European Council of June 2012, that the heads of state and government decided to proceed to what they had hitherto rejected with horror: embarking on banking union. This was the first structural decision fit to resolve a structural problem. How much lost time and how many millions of unemployed might have been avoided, had this decision been taken in 2010? It was the first significant decision towards completing the euro. In fact, if taken to its conclusion, banking union would introduce unified supervision, a unified mechanism for resolving bank failures, and unified insurance of deposits. Such are the institutions of an integrated banking system, where governments will logically be divested of their prudential responsibilities in favour of federal bodies for what are deemed to be systemic banks (those whose collapse would threaten the whole financial sector). We shall see in Chapter 5 how this process might succeed.

At present, banking union is still lopsided. It has progressed in the area of supervision, but less so or not at all in other areas. The most important decision for finally exposing bank losses and for the long-term is that of making the ECB the sole supervisor of the 130 largest banks, but not of the remaining 6,000 banks in the European Union. Nevertheless, it involves a transfer of power to the federal level, enabling a systemic approach to the monitoring of banking risks. Homogeneity in appraising the risks accumulated by one and the same bank, but located in different countries, thus becomes possible. A quality audit of bank assets, appearing on the balance sheet or hidden in off-balance-sheet commitments, must precede the stress tests on which the assessment of recapitalization requirements depends. At the end of this exercise, the ECB has the power to compel banks to recapitalize. Where banks are incapable of so doing by their own means, or by raising capital in the stock market, it would be referred to a resolution authority.

But the SRM (single resolution mechanism), set up following a laborious compromise reached in December 2013 and completed in March 2014, is still far from being operational. In order to fix all kinds of situations, particularly a systemic financial crisis of the 2008 variety, it requires a naturally contingent backstop of public money to recapitalize institutions with insufficient funds of their own, which cannot find the capital required, either on the stock market or via negotiated injections, to restore a sufficiently healthy balance sheet to resume normal activity. Unified resolution therefore signifies fiscal solidarity, contingent on activating the systemic risk inherent in a single financial system. This organic link between banking union and fiscal solidarity has always hitherto been rejected by the Council of heads of state and government. Such rejection is a major obstacle to completing the euro, which requires that the vicious circle between deteriorating public finances and fragility in the banking system be broken. In Chapter 5, I will discuss a possible way of overcoming it. Such a development is not impossible, because progress has been made in the fiscal sphere.

The other major decision of early summer 2012 was to allow the ECB to purchase the government debt of countries in difficulty, obviously under very strict conditions. This is the OMT (Outright Monetary Transactions) programme. It has never been implemented, and probably never will be. But the president of the Board of the ECB, Mario Draghi, proved capable of dextrous use of it. In late July 2012, he solemnly declared that the ECB would do everything in its power to save the euro, and assured the whole world that this would suffice, and that he was ready to purchase government securities if necessary. His speech had the effect of a magic wand. He transformed opinion in the financial markets from dark pessimism to delirious optimism. All financial markets rose without anything having been resolved in the real economy. This episode reveals once again that operators in financial markets have no idea of the economic fundamentals. They are motivated solely by beliefs that are collectively focused on conventions (salient events, speeches by figures regarded as providential, gurus). In fact, the fundamentals are far from having been sorted out. As we saw in Chapter 1, the end of the recession has not given a strong impetus to economies, as a result of which productive investment has continued to decline. Without a strong, prolonged stream of investment to recover the ground lost over five years, there will be no increase in potential growth. That is why the ECB found itself in the front line trying to prevent inflation from falling dangerously, and seeking to revive corporate lending.

On 5 June 2014, after months of equivocation and hesitation when it hoped that the inflation rate would spontaneously correct itself, the ECB's monetary policy committee conceded the danger of unduly low inflation over too long a period. It decided to begin to inflect monetary policy in the eurozone. First of all, the ECB relaunched the LTRO with a four-year term, in a new operation dubbed TLTRO. But this time it confined the facility to banks that lend to the non-financial private sector, excluding credit to households for property purchases. Banks would be able to borrow from the ECB up to 7 per cent of the sum total of their loans in the eligible categories. This manifestly meant favouring the financing of productive investment and consumption. Two operations were envisaged, for September and December 2014, to the tune of 400 billion euros. Extensions would be possible from March 2015 to June 2016. Banks deciding to borrow in this scheme would pay an interest rate of 0.25 per cent, or 10 base points above the key rate. Repayment could be made starting twenty-four months after each transaction.

The ECB lowered its key rate to 0.15 per cent on 5 June 2014. In addition, for the first time it introduced a negative interest rate of –0.10 per cent on bank deposits, on deposits connected to special refinancing operations, and on banks' surplus reserves. Moreover, it further expanded the range of collateral accepted as a guarantee for normal refinancing. Finally, the ECB declared it was preparing the purchase of private securities called asset-backed securities (ABS), which are credits securitized in the non-financial sector, again in order to stimulate the resumption of lending.

The major problem is that the whole operation was tantamount to flogging a dead horse. In launching it, the ECB postulated that banks lacked liquidity for lending to the economy and consequently that, were such liquidity to be available, the amount of credit would increase. But if the malady of the eurozone economy is secular stagnation, aggregate demand in the real economy will not rise. In this case, there will be no more demand for credit with or without TLTRO. Banks will use the new facility to repay old loans from the ECB that are falling due, to the tune of €400 billion, in the old LTRO. This applies above all to Spanish and Italian banks.

In fact, during summer 2014, the economic situation in the eurozone deteriorated sharply. To general surprise, Germany went into recession in the second quarter. The inflation rate continued to drop, from 0.5 per cent in June to 0.3 per cent in August. Italy and Spain tumbled into deflation. On 22 August, during the central bank symposium at Jackson Hole, Wyoming, Mario Draghi made a widely noticed speech. Warning that monetary policy alone could not do everything, he reminded governments of their responsibilities. The only way of escaping the trap of a quasi-zero inflation and double-digit unemployment, he stated, 'is a policy mix that combines monetary, fiscal and structural measures at the union level and at the national level'. That is precisely the position defended in this book. The weakest economies must be reformed by removing obstacles to enterprise and job creation. Countries with room to spend more must do so, while abiding by the rules of the treaty, in order to chart a fiscal course more conducive to growth. Thus, this is an appeal for cooperation between monetary and fiscal policy, in violation of the principles of separation adopted at Maastricht.

For its part, the ECB was not slow to act. In late August, indications that deflationary risks were growing, with a fall in anticipated inflation over five years incorporated into market interest rates, prompted the monetary policy committee to act, without awaiting the results of the measures taken in June, at its meeting of 4 September. The key interest rate was reduced to 0.05 per cent, and a programme launched to purchase private securities in the form of ABS. To be able to operate in sufficient potential volume, the purchase programme was to include not only securities issued on loans to firms and covered bonds, but also securities backed by mortgage loans. Mario Draghi announced the scale of the intended programme: the size of the ECB's balance sheet was to expand from €2 trillion to €3 trillion by adding new purchases of securities and the TLTRO programme of new banking finance. The ball was thus now in the court of governments.

Initiatives in the Fiscal Sphere

Observing that austerity policies had failed, for the reasons explained in Chapter 1, to reverse the increase in government debt as a proportion of countries' GDP, the European Council put in place aid programmes for countries in difficulties. Their administration required the creation of new European financial institutions. The European Financial Stability Fund (EFSF) was a provisional structure created at the onset of the Greek crisis. It was followed by a permanent structure: the European Stability Mechanism (ESM), created on 27 September 2012, which became operational on 1 March 2013.

But that is not all. Just as, in the banking sphere, intergovernmental governance of the eurozone progressed in the direction of completion of the euro, so in the fiscal sphere the European Council, with the exception of the UK and the Czech Republic – hence a larger grouping than the eurozone – agreed on a fiscal pact in January 2012 that was converted into a Fiscal Union Treaty, signed on 2 March. This treaty is also called TSCG (Treaty on Stability, Coordination and Governance).

Firewalls for government finances: the EFSF and ESM

The EFSF is a special, provisional financial vehicle, created following the outbreak of the Greek crisis. It was set up on 7 June 2010 and operated until 30 June 2013, when it made way for the permanent structure of the ESM. It was designed to give assistance to eurozone countries in financial difficulty in the form of loans, banking recapitalization and government debt acquisition. It was financed with €60 billion of loans raised by the European Commission and guaranteed by the European budget, making it possible to borrow €440 billion in the bond market, or a combined arsenal of €500 billion, added to which was €250 billion provided by the IMF. The guarantee was sufficient for the EFSF to borrow with the highest rating.

The EFSF acted as a financial support for a reform programme accepted by the government of a country at bay and imposed by the famous troika – the European Commission, the IMF and the ECB – after acceptance by the Eurogroup. In addition to the balance of Greece's initial rescue plan, and then the totality of the second plan of €110 billion, the EFSF financed programmes for Ireland (€85 billion in January 2011) and Portugal (€78 billion in May–June 2011). After these various instances of assistance, the EFSF's capacity was only €250 billion. So, on 21 June 2011, a capital enlargement was decided on, taking the Fund's liability to €780 billion, and restoring a capacity for effective intervention of €440 billion.

The EFSF was replaced by the ESM, which was able to offer assistance to countries in difficulty from 1 March 2013. This was an international financial institution based in Luxembourg. The structure of its liabilities comprises €80 billion of capital contributed by eurozone member-states and €620 billion borrowed in bond markets. This allows it an assistance lending capacity of €500 billion, complemented by €200 billion of investments in supposedly secure equities – that is, with an AAA rating.

The ESM's creation was met with criticism and, in particular, great suspicion by Germany, which did not oppose its creation but disabled its operation. Criticisms centred on the fundamental political problem faced by Europe in creating federal institutions. It is the product of an intergovernmental agreement that assigns significant financial power to the ESM's governing council without parliamentary control, and therefore without any kind of democratic influence.

The German Constitutional Court stepped into the breech created by this democratic vacuum. It ruled that any new rescue plan involving a eurozone country had to have the prior approval of the Bundestag and be confirmed by the Court. This was to pronounce a kind of extra-territoriality of

Germany's Basic Law, because it was supposed to enunciate civil principles, called eternity clauses, over and above those governing the organization of public powers. This raises the problem of the nature of the fundamental principles that should govern a layered democracy, with national and European levels, which is being constructed by trial and error. This political problem becomes all the greater with fiscal union.

The European Fiscal Union Treaty

This treaty, called the TSCG to indicate its ambitions – stability, coordination, governance – aims to complete the integration of the eurozone. It contains a fiscal pact setting rules for the coordination of fiscal policy. In addition to rules, coordination incorporates procedures for appraisal by independent bodies – the public finance commissions established in each state of the eurozone. This is a major institutional innovation. We shall see in Chapter 7 that it can be used to advance coordination from automatic steering based on rules not contingent on the macroeconomic situation towards a process of cooperation between fiscal decision-making bodies.

The central pillar of the TSCG is the Fiscal Compact, which requires member countries to pass legislation requiring each of them to have a budget in balance or surplus, as defined by the treaty. The national legal arrangements that incorporate the treaty must stipulate a corrective mechanism to prevent deviations.

The treaty defines a balanced budget as one with an actual deficit below 3 per cent and a structural deficit below 0.5 per cent for countries whose debt level-to-GDP ratio is above 60 per cent, and 1 per cent for the others. Member countries whose debt ratio exceeds 60 per cent must aim on average to reduce their debt by one-twentieth each year. Progress towards balance is a medium-term objective. It defines the path of sustainability, according to the treaty. Structural balance is the reference-point for judging this progress. Any annual overshoot must prompt a correction whose temporality, means and scale are determined by the European Commission. Failure to satisfy the obligations of adjustment can result in a fine up to 0.1 per cent of GDP imposed by the European Court of Justice, because respect for the treaty rule comes under the Court's jurisdiction.

This treaty, strongly supported by Germany, is therefore more restrictive than the old stability pact. Only countries that ratify it are eligible for ESM emergency finance. Annual budget plans must be compatible with the stability programme in the medium term. If the 3 per cent deficit threshold is exceeded, the Commission proposes corrective measures, taking account of country-specific sustainability risks.

In spring 2010, the German government interpreted the need for fiscal union as the enactment of a balanced budget law to reform the old Stability and Growth Pact, which had proved its inadequacy. In March 2011, the idea of automatic sanctions for failure to observe the rules on deficits and government debt emerged in the Council's debates. With the escalation of the crisis, the eurozone countries agreed on the need for a new intergovernmental treaty on 9 December 2011. At the European Council summit on 30

January 2012, all countries, with the exception of the United Kingdom and Czech Republic, accepted the Fiscal Pact.

The treaty was signed on 2 March 2012, and was due to come into force on 1 January 2013, depending on ratification by at least twelve signatory countries. After ratification, each country had to incorporate a balanced budget rule into its fiscal law.

Aside from the creation of a public finance council in those countries that did not yet have one, another procedural innovation was the establishment of the European Semester. Fiscal measures are discussed and approved by national parliaments in the autumn. The treaty introduced a shuttling back and forth between national level and European level from the spring onwards. This provides for examination of each country's budget by the European Commission. In addition, governments do not stick to an annual finance law. They are required to develop and present stabilization programmes for the medium term (five years), setting out what is required of fiscal policy to conform to the treaty, or at least approximate to it. These medium-term stabilization programmes are appraised by the European Commission, and give rise to exchanges with the governments. In itself, this procedure is an advance, because it obliges national governments and parliaments to develop a strategic view of budgets. Annual finance laws must be such that structural developments follow the midterm economic trajectory and actual developments fluctuate around it, depending on the gap between potential and actual production (the output gap), within a range that can be explained in the usual conditions of the conjuncture.

In present conditions, however, these measures and adjustment mechanisms have been severely disrupted by the financial crisis. In most countries, structural budget deficits and government debt are very far removed from the equilibrium values stipulated by the rules of the TSCG. Adjustment is therefore not only a matter of managing cyclical fluctuations. It is necessary to identify possible paths of convergence – what are called budget consolidations – on the prescriptive balances accepted by governments. And there's the rub. Obviously, the treaty cannot be held responsible for the failure of the generalized austerity decided on prior to its introduction. Nevertheless, it maintains the constraint of an adjustment that is unrealistic, because it requires excessively rapid consolidation. We saw in Chapter 1 why this was the case. The failure to solve the problems of the financial system, on the one hand, and the abandonment of full employment in Europe as a primary objective of economic policy, on the other, allow free rein to processes conducive to secular stagnation. While retaining the logic of the requisite adjustment, its duration and the scale of the fiscal effort must be revised, relating it to macroeconomic developments that might reasonably be anticipated.

Let us recall that the structural deficit is the level of deficit that would obtain if the economic cycle did not exist. It is therefore the annual average budget deficit or surplus one would expect to find over the whole cycle. This golden rule is contingent on an ordinary economic cycle, certainly not on the need to escape Japanese-style stagnation in economies constrained by private debt reduction. Above all, it is incompatible with the need to reverse the long-term tendency for potential growth to fall.

Thus it is the very definition of the norms – the core of the Stability Pact – that is the problem. As defined, structural balance incorporates all expenditure, including public investment. The budget balance to be respected (a maximum deficit of 0.5 per cent of GDP in practice means balance) entails that public investment must be self-financed by current receipts. With such a financial constraint, one cannot hope for a dynamic, innovative economy, especially given that, as Figure 1.2 showed (p. 28), public investment has collapsed in the eurozone.

If restoring strong growth is a key objective in order to safeguard the European project, and if public investment is (as Scandinavian experience has shown) a growth factor, then the golden rule as currently defined is incongruous. In fact, investment means tomorrow's receipts being higher than today's. It is therefore anti-economical to make today's receipts bear the burden of investment whose duration might be several decades. It amounts to abolishing the intergenerational transfer involved in government debt. In addition, because it increases the growth rate – and hence future fiscal receipts – investment is self-financing, if one is prepared to wait long enough, that is if the state has a strategic plan worthy of the name.

The fiscal rule should therefore be rewritten to make it compatible with an economics of growth, not stagnation – in other words, the economically viable rule that is compatible with the medium-term sustainability of the public finances:[3] *Sustainable structural deficit = net public sector investment adjusted for debt depreciation due to target inflation*. Inflation reduces the real value of any debt expressed in nominal terms. The issue is target inflation, because it is what corresponds to the definition of the structural budget balance. The latter is what we would have if GDP was at its potential level, which is on a path compatible with the validation of anticipated medium-term inflation, hence with expectations in line with the Central Bank's medium-term target.

It therefore allows the state to go into debt to finance investment that produces public goods. The adjustment needed to respect this dynamic equilibrium must take account of the output gap and the gap relative to target inflation: *real deficit = structural deficit – (1/2) (output gap) – (1/2) (actual inflation – target inflation).*

The government deficit must be equal to net public investment augmented by debt depreciation for target inflation, adjusted by a percentage (corresponding to the effect of automatic stabilizers) of the gap between GDP and potential GDP and a percentage of the gap between inflation and its target. The last two elements express the requisite conjunctural flexibility. First of all, when the economy is at the low point of the cycle, the output gap is negative, which justifies a higher government deficit. Next, at the stage of overheating, it is important on the contrary to reconstitute resources by a surplus that makes it possible to respect the structural balance over the whole cycle. Finally, a situation in which interest rates are higher than the rate of nominal growth, as a result of anticipated inflation above the medium-term norm, justifies greater fiscal stringency. Conversely, when an expectation of unduly low inflation indicates underlying deflationary forces, fiscal expansion can counter them. In this way, fiscal policy and monetary policy cooperate to combat a slump and close the output gap. Fiscal policy sustains total demand without threatening medium-term dynamic equilibrium; monetary policy reduces interest rates so that they remain lower than the growth rate, and thus reinforces the sustainability of government debt.

In current conditions, with inflation very considerably below the target of 2 per cent and growth that is almost zero, reasonable fiscal policy would be an ambitious, coordinated programme of public investment, financed by a bond issue guaranteed by the whole eurozone, doubling the rate of public investment as a proportion of GDP, which has fallen to 2 per cent.

3.

Which Handicaps Have Been Exacerbated in the Eurozone?

Chapter 2 revealed the key to understanding the eurozone's woes: the incompletion of the euro. I have shown why and how Europe's economic situation deteriorated, causing it to lose ground compared with the rest of the world since the financial crisis. In this chapter, I will address why and how the incompletion of the euro, which is its original sin, led to an accumulation of structural defects in the eurozone prior to the crisis. In terms of competitiveness, it has accentuated the difference between the member-states. Relatedly, it has polarized creditor and debtor financial positions between countries, which became so many sites of weaknesses in finance and sources of disagreements between governments when the crisis erupted.

Monetary union is a project of political economy. However, it has not been pursued as a fundamental objective, but as a means to other economic and political ends. The economic objective, pursued since the origins of the European project, is economic and financial integration. The other objective was safeguarding the minimal political unity of Europe, after Chancellor Helmut Kohl had unilaterally decided to pursue German reunification at breakneck speed.

The objective of progressive economic integration, conceived as a conjoint transformation of economic structures and institutions, had produced European institutions for regulating competition. This process of cooperation between the member-states was termed *la démarche communautaire*. It was severely disrupted by the disappearance of the Bretton Woods system and by the two oil shocks that left Europe disarmed in the face of the massive international monetary troubles of the 1970s. Economic integration cannot survive exchange-rate variations between the currencies of the participating countries, which make the relative prices of tradeable goods unpredictable and volatile. That is why Chancellor Helmut Schmidt and President Valéry Giscard d'Estaing agreed on the creation of the European Monetary System (EMS) in 1979. However, while it made it possible to salvage what had been achieved in past integration, the EMS was inadequate for the purposes of further progress. In the mid 1980s, Europe risked being caught between two stools. That is why, in 1985, Jacques Delors, then president of the European Commission, proposed furthering integration by extending it to finance. This resulted in the Single European Act, which came into force on 1 January 1987. Henceforth relations between the currencies of member-states were different in kind, because countries began to dismantle their controls on capital movements. The project of creating a single currency developed as the indispensable monetary basis of a unified financial area.

The political shock of German reunification supervened just as this project was developing. The enormous expenditure occasioned by the absorption of the GDR into the Federal Republic soon plunged the EMS into crisis, reinforcing the need for stronger monetary cooperation in order to fulfil the Single Act. At the same time, the French political class was very anxious about a political upheaval that might place Germany in a hegemonic position in Europe as a whole, by extending its domination to the east. That is why President Mitterrand wanted to tether Germany to the European Union via the currency. What ensued was the Kohl–Mitterrand compromise, whereby France unreservedly accepted German unification while Germany abandoned the Deutschmark. This compromise paved the way for the Maastricht Treaty, which was adopted in December 1991, signed in February 1992, and ratified during 1992.

The Maastricht Treaty established an incomplete currency, in the sense described in Chapter 2. The issue of the separation between the currency and state budgets soon arose in the run-up to the introduction of the euro. German leaders were convinced that fiscal policy, and probably economic policy as a whole, should be coordinated. That is why, in 1994, the president of the CDU, Karl Lamers, presented French leaders with a proposal for common economic government, which could be the model for a future economic government of the eurozone. So monolithic is the French conception of sovereignty that the proposal was not even discussed, either in the government or in political parties. That is why Germany's leaders put intense pressure on their partners to get them to adopt binding fiscal rules that would prevent excessive deficits. This was the Stability Pact adopted in Amsterdam on 17 June 1997. It sealed the incompletion of the euro in advance.

However, it was thought that the main thing had been achieved with the creation of the euro: a financial area unified by a single currency. Political cooperation was renounced as finance was placed in command. The hope of political leaders and the civil servants of the European Commission was that these institutions would foster genuine convergence between economies, and that this would make the eurozone 'the most advanced knowledge economy in the world', as the European Council trumpeted in Lisbon in 2000.

We now need to understand why and how the opposite occurred. Nominal convergence between interest rates as a result of financial unification led to a real divergence between economies. Rather than being distributed equitably on the ground, industrial activity was polarized, resulting in the deindustrialization of one part of Europe to the benefit of the other. Surplus and deficit positions crystallized in balances of payments. Persistent divergences in competitiveness took root within the eurozone. In exclusively diffusing a doctrine of competition, and evincing hostility to any form of industrial policy, the spirit of the Single Act exacerbated the many differences between countries.

Real divergences were evident in costs and prices, in the first instance. But they went much further. In order to register them, we must turn to the sources of productivity in innovation systems.

Divergences in the Eurozone: Costs and Prices

In France, managerial circles and their henchmen in the economics profession succeeded in influencing the media:

it was all down to labour costs! Reduce wages, and employers' social overheads and employment would flourish. This rhetoric was adopted by the European Commission. It won over the French government, which could only conceive of one policy: reducing firms' costs. However, we saw in Chapter 1 that investment fell continuously, and productivity stagnated for five years throughout the eurozone. Do not those who determine the allocation of resources – the directors of international finance – share some of the blame? In countries where there was an excessive increase in wages after the euro's advent, what did it result from?

The cumulative divergence in the eurozone stemmed from the same cause that led to the financial crisis: the deregulation of Western finance, which strayed ever further from its proper role – financing the economy – to enjoy the delights of manipulating financial markets. In effect, the process of convergence in Europe hoped for by the 'Lisbon strategy' was left entirely to financial unification, amplified by fiscal competition. No policy of European cooperation to invest in innovation was conceived to support the claim to be global 'leader' in the knowledge economy in 2011.

The virtuous path imagined by the officials of the Commission, and proclaimed by political leaders, is depicted in Figure 3.1a.

The fall in nominal rates in countries projected to converge with Germany on joining the euro, and which did indeed converge, was supposed to prompt capital inflows facilitating a catch-up in the productivity, and hence competitiveness, of these countries, through a massive effort of productive investment in sectors open to international competition.

Chapter 3
Figure 3.1: Macroeconomic Repercussions
of the Introduction of the Euro
3.1a: Imaginary Virtuous Dynamic of the Lisbon Strategy

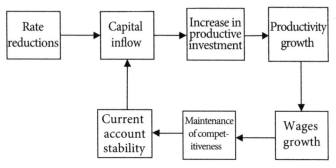

3.1b: Actual Vicious Dynamic of Financial Expansion

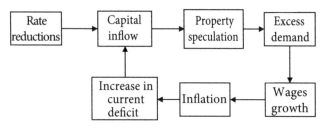

The negative spiral actually generated was, on the contrary, a gigantic speculative bubble, which caused the divergence of the 'peripheral' countries experiencing it. This divergence resulted in their pronounced financial vulnerability, which itself amplified the crisis. If we turn to Spain, for example, where unemployment rose to 25 per cent, the prior rise in wages was entirely down to the absurd excrescence of the property sector.

Property prices: the main factor in divergence between economies

The property sector has played a decisive role in European imbalances.

The rise in property prices was both cause and consequence of the increase in debt. It not only contributed to household debt, but also distorted corporate investment decisions. On the one hand, the cost of property services impacted on production costs in France and Spain, for example, whereas prices and rents did not rise in Germany. On the other hand, the increase in property prices encouraged a hike in wages.

Figure 3.2 shows the enormous divergence between Germany, on the one hand, and France and Spain, on the

Figure 3.2: Property Price Indicators
in Four European Countries

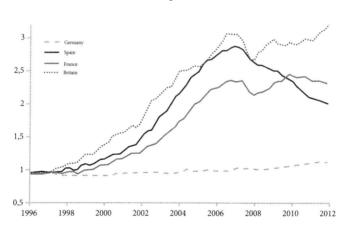

Source: ECB, compilation of national indicators

other. Property prices did not shift in Germany, whereas they exploded in Spain and rose significantly in France, where they remained on a very high plateau after the onset of the financial crisis.

We can now see how the vicious circle in Figure 3.1b was generated. The differential property dynamic led to divergent inflation rates between countries, whereas nominal rates had converged. Between 1999 and 2012, the average annual inflation rate was 0.9 per cent in Germany, 1.7 per cent in France, and 2.6 per cent in Spain. As a result, real interest rates fell most in countries where property prices rose most, and lending surged, since the real interest rate determines the cost of credit. It is difficult to conceive of a more inefficient form of financial self-regulation. But governments saw nothing, and did not want to see anything. As for the ECB – it had no mandate to intervene in finance! The process of divergence therefore persisted, rather than inducing compensatory adjustments. We can now see that monetary union without coordinated economic policy, and without prudential regulation worthy of the name, is directly implicated, because it ensured the equalization of nominal interest rates and nothing else. France did not experience an explosive rise in debt, because the deposit required for property purchases remained reasonable. Nevertheless, there was a drift in the direction of property prices remaining high.

Divergence in labour costs

We have just seen the main reason for the divergence between economies. The second reason consists in the peculiarity of Germany: the inflationary legacy of unification and an ultra-restrictive policy to eradicate it. So the divergence in wage costs is not, as is too often believed, an explosion of variations in labour costs in all directions. It is a case of Germany, on the one hand, and all other countries, on the other. This is also true when we add in the UK and the United States. Furthermore, the true measure of competitiveness is not labour costs: it is unit costs – that is, costs per unit produced. Figure 3.3 provides a relative measure of levels starting from a base of one for all countries in 1995. It is therefore the best measure of the way that a country's competitiveness has diverged from its principal partners within Western economies as a result of the development of wages.

Figure 3.3: Development of Countries' Competitiveness,
Measured by Weighted Unit Wage Costs

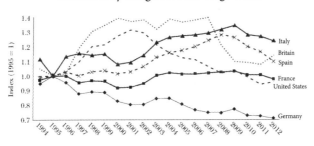

Source: Dustmann, Fitzenberger, Schönberg
and Spitz-Oener (2014)

What clearly emerges is that Germany is completely atypical. Spain and the United Kingdom are the European countries that have suffered the most violent speculative waves in property: wages soared, and then fell back, with property prices. By contrast, real estate speculation in the

United States was caused by the crisis in so-called sub-primes. But neither the rise in property prices nor their fall influenced wage costs. It was the stock market bubble of 1996–2001, involving the so-called 'new economy', that did that. The inflation of wage costs was gradually brought down thereafter. For its part, France did not experience any jolts in wage costs. Its competitiveness cost remained average.

The lessons to be drawn from this indicate how the French government erred in its 'supply-side' policy. The latter was solely concerned with wage costs. We shall see in Chapter 4 that the French productive system in fact weakened throughout the years 1998–2012 against most other Western economies. This is manifestly not attributable, either entirely or chiefly, to labour costs. Given the results of Figure 3.2, would it not be more expedient to look to property income?

In addition, we shall have to ask what, precisely, imitating Germany would entail. It is reminiscent of the 1980s, when Japan posted exceptional export performances and the rhetorical fashion was to express a desire to imitate Japan. This is absurd: Germany is inimitable precisely because it is exceptional. But this will not last, any more than it did in Japan. Germany suffers from a major demographic handicap, which is already a factor in very weak final demand. It will not be long before it poses a problem of labour supply, especially given that profound social conservatism about female labour, combined with the weakness of public services for pre-school children, neuters part of the potential labour force. It is doubtful whether the forthcoming labour shortage can be completely offset by continued immigration. Moreover, Germany is a country with low levels of investment, above all in infrastructure. German economic success rests on the non-price competitiveness of the *Mittelstand* in the manufacturing industry. Germany's excellence in producing machine tools and specialist equipment for construction and consumer durables is peerless. But Chinese demand for such imports is slowing markedly, and it is far from clear that other emergent or developing countries will take up the slack.

What do Germany's exceptional characteristics consist of? If we stick to wage costs, it is very clear: services (Figure 3.4). This is an indirect consequence of German reunification, which supplied the economy with a large quantity of skilled labour previously employed in enterprises with obsolete technology. Thus, this pertains to exceptional causes. At one and the same time, there was pressure on wages through labour competition and a leap in productivity through the transfer of this labour into modern enterprises.[1] It was from 1995 onwards that the relative decline in unit wage costs occurred (Figure 3.3). The break occurred in 1995, in services, and not in 2004–05, during Gerhard Schröder's anti-wage policy. Like Figure 3.3, however, Figure 3.4 does not register France's divergence from the other countries of the eurozone (excluding Germany). It is Germany that is exceptional. The question is whether it is reasonable to endeavour to imitate a partner that has enjoyed an exceptional advantage over the last twenty years, especially when that advantage can be attributed to characteristics (unit wage costs in industry) that are not among the most relevant.

Figure 3.4: Unit Labour Costs in Services in the OECD

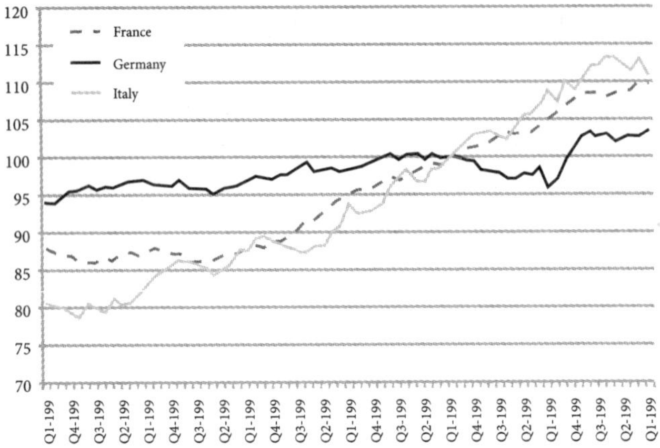

Source: Eurostat

The mystery of the price of corporate services

A change in systems of production over the last thirty years has been the outsourcing of numerous tasks formerly integrated into industrial enterprises. This phenomenon accentuates differences in industrial competitiveness if costs in services develop differently. According to Eurostat, France is in an exceptional position in Europe as regards the share in value added of services outsourced to enterprises in total value added in industry (excluding construction) and corporate services. In 2012, it reached 50 per cent in France, compared with 30 per cent in Germany, and 35 per cent on average in the eurozone. Worse, the French position continued to diverge from 2000.

The anomaly is, in the first instance, the result of price stability in corporate services in Germany, as indicated by Figure 3.4, whereas prices have regularly risen much more in

France than in other eurozone countries. We know that France is the country par excellence of protected markets of all kinds, from pharmacists to taxi drivers. This is particularly pronounced in corporate services. Financialization has led to the proliferation of legal services, consultants, sellers of financial products, informants and assessors of all kinds, whose incomes are particularly high. Being largely dependent upon Anglo-American institutional shareholders, French enterprises have plentiful recourse to them. The anomaly also derives from a more disturbing development. The price of industry's value added stagnated from 2008, reflecting French industry's problems in producing high value-added goods. This leads us to the heart of the problems of competitiveness, which go far beyond the issue of labour costs.

Divergences in the Eurozone: Competitiveness and Industrial Dynamics

A naive conclusion might be drawn from the preceding results: if high value added is to be found in services, then let's produce services and abandon industry! Such was the UK's option for financial services in the 1980s. But the German example is the opposite, where services are ingredients for improving industrial productivity. We must therefore extend the analysis and understand what is meant by a developed country's competitiveness and what industry is in today's world.

The technological progress measured by the overall productivity of factors also evinces clear signs of intra-European differences. Unlike the microeconomic competitiveness of enterprises, the macroeconomic competitiveness of nations is a notion that makes no sense in the standard theory of comparative advantages. Since the latter is relative and supposed to be exogenous, it always exists and is always realized in a system of international free trade, because the relative equilibrium prices of goods sold in international commerce are fixed at levels that signal these advantages to consumers. Whether a country has high or low wages, it will be relatively more successful in activities appropriate to the relative income level that its endowments in factors of production enable it to attain.

For macroeconomic competitiveness to be meaningful, comparative advantages must be endogenous and potentially cumulative. This is the case if international specialization is based on growing output and drivers of agglomeration that generate self-reinforcing processes and external effects. If enterprises become more efficient due to tacit exchanges of information and skills with other firms situated nearby, or thanks to pooling research investment or joint participation in programmes conducted in public research laboratories, then overall competitiveness has meaning. It results from a composition effect in performance attributable to corporate strategies in the context of impetus from public policy. A complex coordination problem then arises. The success of such coordination can result at the macroeconomic level in the following schema, which is a virtuous circle of productivity and growth, called the Kaldor-Verdoorn law (Figure 3.5).

Innovation depends upon corporate investment in R&D. But the picture is very mixed in Europe. In Southern Europe it is dramatically inadequate (between 0.5 and 0.8 per cent of GDP). Since 2002, R&D in the private sector has never

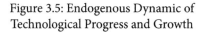

Figure 3.5: Endogenous Dynamic of
Technological Progress and Growth

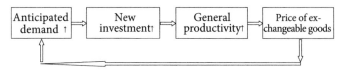

exceeded 1.4 per cent in France, compared with 1.9 per cent
on average in Germany, 2 per cent in the United States, 2.5
per cent in Japan and 2.8 per cent in Sweden. Furthermore,
French enterprises increasingly lag behind in the automation
of industrial production processes. French enterprises
bought 3.5 times fewer industrial robots than Germany in
2001 and seven times fewer in 2011. Studies of the general
productivity of factors indicate that the antiquity of capital
in French enterprises is a factor in productivity slowdown,
since capital renewal is too slow.

This puts the issue of national competitiveness in a
different light. For supply and demand are interdependent
in determining long-term growth, contrary to the standard
theory, which assumes exogenous comparative advantages,
determined by what is called 'factor endowments'. In a sense,
Figure 3.5 is the antidote to the process of secular stagnation
represented in Figure 3.4 (p. 72). Demand is crucial here,
with the incorporation of new products into modes of
consumption. This involves a dynamic development of real
incomes closely linked to productivity gains.

We arrive at the following definition of national
competitiveness: a country that is more competitive than
another country is one that exports goods with high-value
national labour to the world market and imports goods

with lower-value foreign labour, when these values are expressed in the same accounting unit. It can be encapsulated in a cursory formula: being competitive is selling national labour expensively on the world market. In a globalized universe, the relevant demand is global demand. A country can sell its labour expensively if it possesses an industrial specialization such that its exports are largely unaffected by variations in relative prices. It will then be said to possess good non-price competitiveness.

The available econometric estimates of export functions suggest that the elasticity of exports in response to the variation in real effective exchange rates is significantly lower in Germany than in France: −0.4 per cent as against −0.9 per cent, respectively. This means that a 1 per cent reduction in price competitiveness, measured overall, reduces exports by 0.9 per cent in France compared with 0.4 per cent in Germany. A country with high non-price competitiveness thus has enterprises that can sustain profitable prices – that is, protect their profit margins despite foreign competition. This cannot be done by the enterprises of a country vulnerable to cost differences. A high, stable profit margin provides resources for investing without going too far into debt, and hence for increasing productivity and potential growth – that is, maintaining the virtuous circle of growth and competitiveness. From this, the public authorities and corporate directors should conclude that salvation consists in productivity gains to improve non-price competitiveness. Yet the former are engaged in an attempt to drive down wage costs compared with the countries of southern Europe, with Spain becoming the new model. As to the latter, they dream of dismantling labour laws so as to fall into line with the conditions of exploitation of labour in emerging countries, emulating the UK. Or, if they have the means, they quite simply abandon the home territory.

Consequences: balance-of-payments divergences and industrial polarization

The structural differences analysed in this chapter have highlighted the contrast between Germany and its partners. They are reflected in the balance of payments, at a time when the eurozone as a whole is in the grips of secular stagnation (Table 1).

Table 3.1: GDP Growth and Current Account Average 2008–13

Country	Growth (average annual percentage)	Current balance (percentage of GDP)
Germany	0,7	+ 6,7
France	0,1	- 1,7
Italy	- 1,5	- 1,9
Spain	- 1,0	- 3,9
Eurozone	- 0,3	+ 1,0

Source: Calculations based on IMF, *World Economic Growth*, April 2014, Statistical Appendix, Table A2 and A11.

These are developments over the course of six years. They therefore depict the medium term, not the conjuncture. On the one hand, growth has everywhere come to a dramatic halt. Germany only emerged relatively unscathed because of its exports. Domestic demand was as anaemic as elsewhere. The polarization of current accounts indicates the lack of cooperation in the eurozone. Of major countries,

Germany has by far the highest current surplus in the world – a surplus that rose to 7.5 per cent of GDP in 2013 and over 9 per cent in 2016. In light of its partners' deficits, such a surplus indicates the scale of the prevalent contrast in Europe, the result of the industrial polarization in Germany's favour. Above all, it reveals the insufficiency of its domestic demand. Germany has the resources to improve its population's well-being, while aiding its partners' adjustment.

But the German industrial machine is export-orientated, whereas economic policy functions to amass maximum financial assets over other countries, including European partners. This confirms the findings of Chapter 1. The euro's incompletion results in member countries constraining one another, with Germany finding an escape route in demand from the rest of the world. But why has German industry benefited so much from creation of the eurozone?

The geographical theory of economics – that is, of the location of economic activities on particular sites – helps us to understand why, and would have helped us to anticipate what would occur, if the forces of integration were left to their own devices without a European industrial policy to orient them.[2] I have already outlined the process generating endogenous comparative advantages (Figure 3.5). It is based on the increasing returns inherent in industrial specialization. The latter leads to spatial concentration, which benefits from agglomeration effects yielding increasing returns. Economies of scale (increasing returns) and agglomeration effects are mutually sustaining, in a virtuous circle of increased productivity and growth in the industrial pole's market shares of available demand.

When the eurozone was created, the size of the internal

market increased enormously to coincide with that of the monetary zone, since the prices of tradable goods were equalized. German industry, which was already the strongest in Europe and had seen its domestic market grow with reunification, was able to benefit from returns to scale in an area of 300 million inhabitants. That is why, far from becoming homogenous, the eurozone became more and more heterogeneous in terms of industrial competitiveness. The differences in competitiveness between the Northern countries, located in the German orbit, and the Southern countries have only grown since creation of the euro.

But, it will be said, the economy of the future is a service economy. The cards are therefore going to be entirely reshuffled. The knowledge economy is based on immaterial capital and activities. But the latter are intimately bound up with material production. They have high fixed costs and marginal costs that decrease with the size of the material production to which they are linked. Superior services are also the nuclei of concentration, because highly skilled human capital requires cooperation to supply complex, customized services. Economies of scale are not reduced. On the contrary, they are reinforced by economies of calibre.

How is the French economy to position itself in the face of these changes, given the impairment it has suffered in the last decade and the legacy of the crisis?

The Deleterious Impact of Structural Divergences on the Eurozone's Cohesion and the Political Risks

In a monetary union, the existence of structural asymmetries between countries poses tricky problems of adjustment, for they are the breeding-ground in which dynamic divergences emerge in the conjuncture. Abiding differences ensue in terms of growth, inflation, employment and the balance of payments. They persist because countries do not have the recourse of varying exchange rates to adjust their relative positions through changes in relative prices and their effects on foreign trade. The belief that internal relative prices can replace exchange-rate adjustment is a dangerous illusion. The idea is to lower wages in countries in deficit and debt. But are they to rise in countries in surplus and credit, to make such adjustment tolerable? If every country is out for itself, countries in surplus are under no compulsion to do so. Adjustment is asymmetrical and ruinous.

The problem has long been familiar. It is a basic lesson of international economics. In a monetary union, everyone for himself leads to an inefficient equilibrium (the Nash equilibrium). Because adjustment via exchange rates is excluded, costly asymmetries must be corrected by flows of relative demand, coordinating the means of economic policy. This means that all countries would enjoy a better position in terms of growth, income and jobs if they coordinated with one another and the central bank on a cooperative equilibrium. In the eurozone, this is impeded by bad governance. What prevents such equilibrium in the framework of intergovernmental governance is that everyone defends their own interests, while taking those of others for granted. No reciprocal adjustment in the direction of a shared interest is attainable. The ECB alone articulates a common interest. But it can only concern itself with the eurozone's average condition. Reciprocal adjustments lie beyond its reach. That is what Mario Draghi means when he says that it cannot do everything.

In a monetary union like the eurozone, where one country is economically dominant and best approximates to a satisfactory macroeconomic equilibrium, a better configuration than the Nash equilibrium would be possible if Germany displayed leadership. This is a benevolent hegemonic equilibrium (the so-called Stackelberg equilibrium). Exercising benevolent leadership means acting while taking account of the interests of the whole zone, provided that the other countries make the adjustments assigned to them. Germany, which had an average surplus of 6.7 per cent on its current account in 2008–13, 7.5 per cent in 2013, and 9 per cent in 2016, would have to use its excess savings to invest, and/or reduce it by consuming more, particularly by increasing the incomes of disadvantaged social categories. In this way, the surplus would decrease, growth would be stronger, the great mass of workers in part-time work out of necessity could work more, and the real wages of the 60 per cent of workers who are least well-paid could rise a little, whereas they have fallen since 2000. Germany would thrive, and its enhanced dynamism would help other countries implement fiscal adjustment without succumbing to deflation.

But Germany sees itself as a big Switzerland. It obstinately rules out any idea of leadership. Political debate in Germany is not irrelevant to this. It is dominated by a highly influential conservative ideological current in a culture profoundly rooted in idolatrous respect for predetermined, inflexible rules. This ideology has fashioned a moral conception of economic problems. In it, debt is a transgression. Countries that borrowed too much prior to the crisis (financed by German banks!) are responsible for their situation, and must make amends by expiating their sin through unemployment and deflation.

Added to this expiatory view of economic adjustment is the illusion that Germany does not need Europe because its ability to export to a rapidly growing emerging world will last indefinitely. Yet globalization is in the process of changing in kind. Countries whose emergence derived from very strong growth pulled along by exports to a West running up debts left, right and centre – hence, countries importing the machine tools that Germany excels in producing – that is already yesterday's world. Globalization is following a different course. The emerging countries are engaged in a perilous transition to transform their domestic economies. They are themselves becoming sources of technological innovation. Economic integration is restructuring trade on regional bases and as regards the supply of raw materials. The interlocking of the production of material goods and the digital revolution is nurturing sources of technological advancement in which German enterprises are not dominant. All these developments are going to require considerable adaptation from the developed countries, whose effectiveness for Europeans depends on interdependent innovation policies across the whole Union.

More worrying still is the fall in investment in Germany, and the consequent mediocrity of productivity gains.[3] The rate of investment in Germany has dipped from 23 to 17 per cent in twenty years. Public investment has hit rock-bottom, incapable of renewing a dilapidated infrastructure. Added to this handicap are demographic and social problems. The demographic situation is worrying in the long term, with a declining population and very low fertility rates that do not portend any recovery. Compounding this is a burdensome social conservatism, smothering the potential that would be realized by promoting women in the labour market. The latter is marked by a dualism that creates profound wage inequalities, by poverty that is spreading despite the economy's apparent good health, and by the blocking of opportunities for social mobility for disadvantaged families.

If Germany's future lies in the success of the European project, as did its post-war renaissance, its refusal to cooperate should not result in the destruction of the euro, which is the most advanced realization of Europe. Yet the lack of cooperation in the adjustment dictated by distortions resulting from the eurozone's financial crisis is incubating political risks, which it would be a mistake to underestimate. Even if we exclude the authoritarian developments with fascist connotations in Hungary, aspirations to political subdivision in Spain, and especially the rise of populism in France as aberrations, there are dangers for the future of Europe. These political risks are the direct effect of the shortcomings in European governance on account of conflict-ridden relations between governments.

Because political leaders have proved incapable of equipping monetary union with the common political institutions that would have made the euro a complete currency, this entity has none of the democratic legitimacy that might give the citizens of member countries a sense of belonging, and hence cohesion of a political kind. It follows that the eurozone can only distinguish itself by its economic performance. Yet this depends directly on the economic policy coordination that is prevented by conflicts of interest between states. Thus, there is growing rejection by citizens as their governments pile up promises they are incapable of keeping. That is why scenarios deemed inconceivable a short while ago are now not unlikely, and are becoming more likely as long as enduring stagnation sets in. Such a scenario concerns France, first and foremost.

France has avoided the worst. Consider the scenario that was feared in the Spring of 2017. Let us suppose that the slump lasted in France until 2017. The National Front arrives in power via the presidential election. The stupidity of the French Constitution gives it a legislative majority immediately afterwards, possibly through an electoral pact with the party of the traditional right in the wake of the breakup of the right-wing party. Marine Le Pen, president of the Republic, takes three economic policy decisions: closure of borders to immigration, abandonment of the euro and restoration of the franc, and an expansionary fiscal policy to eradicate unemployment. Inflation would soon have emerged, followed by authoritarian price controls in an attempt to subdue it.

The shock would have reverberated throughout Europe. To prevent the depreciation of the franc turning into an inflationary spiral, the introduction of capital controls would have been indispensable. The single market in financial services would have disappeared, and the whole European Union would have been affected by fragmentation. The shock wave would have spread throughout Europe. A bloc around Germany might have reconstituted itself as Northern Europe. In Southern Europe, countries (or some countries) with close links to France would have had an interest in following the same path in monetary terms, even if they do not share the same political ideology. Given such a sequence of events, Europe might have regressed by several decades before its construction is put back on track.

In Chapter 7, I shall indicate potential institutional developments that would make it possible to advance cooperation in economic policy rapidly, so as to avoid such a nightmare scenario. But let us first examine France's economic condition.

4.

Does France Have a
Particular Impairment?

The decline in French industry's competitiveness has become a leitmotif. Economists who have the ear of the authorities advocate a 'supply shock' to halt it. This has been interpreted by the government as a policy of reducing wage costs coupled with a tax credit, grandiosely dubbed 'for competitiveness and employment', and generously distributed to all enterprises while urging them to use it to invest. The question is as follows: Can a reduction in wage costs create the virtuous circle of innovatory investment and recovery in the general productivity of factors, represented in Figure 3.5?

In truth, government policy is hit-and-miss. It does not really involve a massive reduction in wage costs, as implemented by Spain, because the government fears an additional drop in household demand. There is therefore little chance of it significantly improving price competitiveness compared with our neighbours. Furthermore, it is a policy that does not deal with the key problem of non-price competitiveness.

The French economy's problem in fact revolves around weak progress in the general productivity of factors on account of a slowdown in the productivity of industrial labour, the reduction of the weight of industry in the economy, and the stagnation of productivity in services. In Chapter 3 I noted the low investment in R&D in French enterprises. The same goes for rates of investment in machines and equipment, in particular evincing a considerable lag in the automation of industrial production processes. In addition, inadequate investment in R&D slows the pace of diffusion of the digital economy.

That is why a multiplicity of approaches is required to identify our economic deficiencies. The first dimension is corporate profitability, if it is granted that profit is at once the motor force in investment decisions and the principal means of effecting it. But we need to go beyond generalities and concern ourselves with different categories of enterprise – SMEs (small and medium-sized enterprises), intermediate-sized enterprises (ISEs), and micro-enterprises – in connection with means of finance. The second dimension is the issue of innovation systems. At the national level, the flow of innovation is not the sum of independent discoveries. Inter-enterprise relations are essential, on condition that they are structured into innovation systems. France is characterized by deficient inter-industrial relations and by a lack of clearly defined innovation systems. The old idea of poles of competitiveness posted some successes, notably in the Rhône-Alpes region, but they were too few and far between. The third dimension of productivity involves social relations within enterprises. France is characterized by a high level of latent conflict in labour relations. Social dialogue is institutionalized, but its content is meagre, in particular because the shareholder principle prevails over the partnership principle in corporate governance. Problems in the labour market flow from this: casualization of wage-earners, downgrading of jobs relative to workers' qualifications, declining social mobility, insufficiently vocational and narrowly compartmentalized forms of education and training. These are dysfunctions that result in growing structural unemployment and social segmentation.

Profitability and the Financialization of Enterprises: The Fragility of SMEs

There is a consensus about the impairment of French enterprises through erosion of their profit margins and capacity for self-financing. However, the phenomenon is far from being homogenous. According to INSEE's national accounts, profit margins for the totality of non-financial companies have only fallen since the financial crisis of 2007. By contrast, they have fallen in the manufacturing industry since the beginning of the century. On the other hand, they have risen significantly in construction. The doubling of margins in this sector, with the increase in property prices, has sustained firms' average profit rate. But the rise in property prices necessitates a hike in wages to cover housing costs as a share of household expenditure. It therefore impacts indirectly on wage costs in the whole economy, and directly on the cost of renting and of real estate services for enterprises in other sectors.

With 2007 as the turning-point, we can compare the development of the profit margins of French enterprises with those of other large or medium-sized European countries over two periods (Table 4.1). As a result of a radically different macroeconomic management of the crisis, growth returned to the United States in 2009, whereas the eurozone was mired in recession after 2010. Spain proceeded to a drastic restructuring through implosion of its surplus real estate, redeployment to industry, and a ferocious attack on wage costs – whence a spectacular restoration of profit margins. For the rest, the fall in margins in France was no anomaly. In particular, it was less sharp than in Germany. It was in the years 2000–07 that Germany made the difference, which resulted partly from the anomaly depicted in Figure 3.3, p. 69, indicating that unit labour costs developed in the opposite direction to all other countries. The second reason was the enormous advance of German exports – more than 10 per cent per annum – in the phase of US economic overheating and Chinese growth. This performance was itself a product of the world economy's unsustainable path coinciding with German industry's excellent non-price competitiveness.

Table 4.1: Comparative Development of Profit Margins of Non-Financial Companies – Percentage

	2000-2007	2007-2012
Germany	+ 7,3	- 4,6
Spain	- 0,7	+ 5,4
France	+ 1,0	- 3,4
Italy	- 3,4	- 4,5
Britain	+ 1,5	- 2,9
United States	+ 4,9	+ 2,7

Source: Eurostat, Bureau of Economic Analysis

The fact that French industry lost ground in a period of high growth, when Figure 3.3 shows that its price competitiveness did not deteriorate compared with countries other than Germany, confirms that French industry's Achilles' heel is non-price competitiveness. In fact, French enterprises' market share in exports compared with foreign demand for goods and services fell from 6 per cent in 1994 to 4 per cent in 2012. The drop is due above all to the fall in the share of goods, as services progressed thanks to tourism.

The particular problem of SMEs

The report of the Observatoire du Financement des Entreprises (OFE) makes possible a more fine-grained analysis of profitability according to enterprise size: SMEs, ISEs, and large enterprises. Figure 4.1 depicts both the close correlation between temporal profiles and the difference in levels of average profit margin between differently sized enterprises. As might be expected, these levels are a function of size.

Profit margins fell with the onset of the crisis. The recovery of 2010 was wiped out by the policy of fiscal austerity, which ended up overcoming the resistance of household consumption, and by banks' reluctance to lend to the economy, as French SMEs export relatively little, being highly dependent on domestic demand. The profit margin of SMEs, which was 23 per cent in 2000, fell to 20.8 per cent in 2012, according to Bank of France data. The drop was scarcely catastrophic. But the profit margin level is greatly inferior to the European average for this category of enterprise.

Figure 4.1: Profit Margin by Size of Enterprise – Percentage

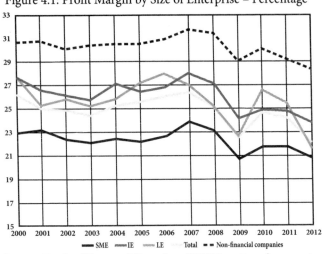

Source: Bank of France, Fiben data; INSEE, national accounts

The OFE goes much further. It studied the distribution of profit margins between enterprises in each class and found that it was highly staggered in all classes. In other words, corporate performance is very mixed. The crisis hit enterprises hardest that were already less successful in the years 2000–07. Profit rates became markedly negative in SMEs and ISEs in the first decile, where we find most of the collapses that have occurred since 2008.

This leads on to the issue of the transition from enterprises' profit margin to their financial condition. The OFE report supplies valuable information. Whereas France occupies an average position among European countries (excluding Spain) for developments in the profit margin of the totality of non-financial companies, this is definitely not the case when it comes to corporate savings (Table 4.2). France is the country where the savings ratio, and hence corporate capacity for self-financing, has deteriorated almost continually since 2000. Despite a constant rise in debt, falling interest rates have contained financial obligations. The central phenomenon is the very pronounced rise in dividends in mid crisis, partially offset by tax reductions. The income transfer involved in financialization encompasses enterprises of all shapes and sizes.

Financialization is boosted by the external growth of enterprises structured as consortiums, in the form of acquisitions and the creation of subsidiaries. This increases debt and creates financial holdings, which lead to dividend payments to the group's financial holding. As a result, financial strategies impact on all sizes of enterprise. Liabilities grow as a proportion of value added for all sizes of enterprise. Financialization thus induces ever greater dependency on debt. That is why the rate of self-financing of French SMEs has fallen massively, from 88 per cent in 2004 to 66 per cent in 2013.

Table 4.2: SME: From Profit to Savings
As a percentage of value added

	2000	2007	2012
Marginal rates	23,1	23,9	20,9
Interest accrued	- 4,4	- 3,8	- 3,7
Dividends paid	- 5,1	- 6,8	- 8,2
Other	0,0	+ 0,8	+ 2,6
Savings ratio	13,6	14,1	11,6

Source: OFE

A high degree of dependency on debt, with widely dispersed profit margins, means that numerous enterprises are in great financial difficulty or even insolvent. Coface has confirmed this observation in its study of the failures of French SMEs.[1] It is striking to see that, in February 2014, the number of French corporate failures was higher than in the 2009 recession. This was no longer a severe conjunctural shock, but an attrition characteristic of secular stagnation. Obviously, such failures have a major impact in job losses and future threats to activity. According to Coface, the number of failures can only be reduced, and the employment situation thereby improved, if GDP growth is at least 1.6 per cent. In 2014, it is unlikely to exceed 0.4 per cent. Utterly inadequate growth; erosion of profitability; increasing indebtedness and collapses – such is the drama of French enterprises, which is far from being primarily attributable to labour costs.

The question that remains to be clarified is this: Where is the highest level of debt to be found? Coface's answer, which coincides with what was said above about financialization, is that corporate failures are bound up more with inter-enterprise financial relations than with traditional banking loans. In February 2014, failing enterprises had a supplier debt almost twice as high as their bank debt. The risk associated with inter-enterprise debt is systemic. It creates a domino effect, since a failing enterprise's unpaid debt to its supplier may be propagated all along the production chain, especially if financial fragility is widespread. The process of serial defaults is difficult to halt, if there is not an enterprise in a sufficiently robust financial situation to absorb the losses.

This is because enterprises connected by inter-industrial exchanges do not form organized systems (innovation systems, clusters, poles of competitiveness, and so on), where mutual guarantees obtain, mediated by the reassurance of financial bodies that form part of the same systems, because the enterprises share the same development project. Here we see the need to recognize that industrial logic, with its agglomeration effects and returns to scale, cannot be efficient if enterprises are connected exclusively by market relations. The technical, informational and financial solidarity afforded by organized innovation systems is lacking. France suffers from inefficient industrial organization. To adopt this industrial logic, however, enterprises are needed whose strategic goals and modes of governance mobilize the creativity of the totality of human resources they contain – and hence are of the partnership variety. This mutation in governance will be discussed in Chapter 8 as the basis of a new social contract, itself an indispensable condition of European revival. The point of this chapter is to demonstrate the ravages of shareholder governance on labour and its productivity.

Financialization and the Harmful Effects of Shareholder Governance

After the Second World War, France modernized under the impetus and guidance of the central state. The tutelary state enabled French capitalism to construct its poles of competitiveness in transport, energy, building materials and chemistry.[2] Following the creation of the Common Market, the industrial model drifted towards more competition, while periodically offsetting deteriorating competitiveness by currency devaluations. European constraints changed the situation when financial liberalization increased. The turn to competitive disinflation in 1983 prompted a passive conversion to Anglo-American neoliberalism.

This ideological movement, advocating corporate governance exclusively in the service of shareholders, developed in the United States in the 1970s and was generalized in the 1980s. It rejected a conception of the enterprise as a private company, legally defined as an autonomous institution, replacing it with one of clusters of implicit contracts. The Chicago theory allocated an exceptional role to shareholders. It made the relationship between shareholders and enterprises one of principal and agent, defining the capitalist enterprise. It maintains that the utility function of shareholders may legitimately be imposed on enterprises. Consequently, in this conception, corporate governance must focus exclusively on achieving shareholders' goals, because all the other relations contributing to the smooth running of enterprises are purportedly contractual. Their remuneration is said to be the equilibrium price that measures their bearers' marginal contributions to the enterprise's value creation.

The conversion of the French financial establishment to this credo occurred from 1995, when the owner of AXA decided that it was time to abandon the system of governance by cross-holdings, which made up the 'hard cores' established by Balladur out of the 1986 privatization wave. The web of cross-capitalist interests disintegrated, and the irruption of Anglo-American shareholders into the CAC 40 turned corporate governance upside down. French capitalism adopted shareholder governance en masse, in contrast to the partnership governance prevalent in Germany. The combination of the prioritization of shareholder-value maximization and a hierarchical, pyramidal organization of labour – an old French tradition – creates managerial incentives especially unconducive to innovative productive investment.

Giving managers an interest in the financial valuation of enterprises, through both stock options and the threat of hostile takeover bids by coalitions of speculative investment funds and investment banks, subjects corporate strategies to the vagaries of stock markets. The stock market becomes the exclusive benchmark institution, and stock-market value the sole representation of shareholders' interests. The consequences for modes of governance are disastrous. The enterprise is no longer regarded as an entity whose integrative capacity is the source of value and must therefore be preserved to develop a strategy of long-term productive investment.[3] In the Wall Street model, the enterprise is nothing more than a collection of assets that can be valued separately on the stock market. Liquidity, not commitment over time, is the primordial quality that investors must be able to reconfigure in order to maximize dividend yields. The total return on shares (dividends + capital gains) is the ground on which financial profit is built.

All market-orientated financial organization pressurizes enterprises to post exorbitant returns on equity, or at any rate returns that bear no relation to productive capital's real capacity for valorization. Financial profit can therefore only be constructed by recourse to increasing debt, which nevertheless remains cheap thanks to the injection of liquidity by central banks – hence the absence of corporate debt reduction in the years following the crisis. Debt makes it possible to reduce capital reserves by repurchasing shares, thereby increasing the leverage of profitability. It also makes it possible to distribute dividends despite economic stagnation.

Dividends, which are supposed to be the unpredictable income par excellence, become guaranteed. As Table 4.2 illustrates, this logic is not confined to large enterprises. The dividends paid by SMEs have grown considerably since 2007.

Finally, debt encourages operations to transfer property through mergers, acquisitions and the re-sale of corporate assets. These operations make considerable stock market gains possible when they are carried out, without corresponding to any clearly defined industrial logic. Consequently, what matters is not holding corporate capital, but rather turnover to realize the financial capital gains made possible by the hustle and bustle of the stock market. Since the onset of the financialization of enterprises, the average term of share-holding has fallen significantly (in the United States from an average of seven years in the late 1960s to seven months in 2007).

It seems reasonable to suppose that such a narrowing of horizons changes what shareholders require of company managers. For governance to be exclusively at the beck and call of shareholders, the interests of managers, which cannot change at the same rate as shareholder turnover, must be aligned with the criterion of maximizing the total return on shares. Such incentives make enterprises subject exclusively to the goal of maximizing the market value of capital stock, disconnecting this from the goal of growth in the economy. This principle results in a more rapid concentration of wealth. The social consequences of this kind of incentive are enormous.

Shareholder governance and negation of the social contract

To claim that shareholders alone are legitimate when it comes to defining corporate goals, and that these goals are validated solely by the stock market, downgrades the other partners in the enterprise, while claiming that their contribution is remunerated exactly in accordance with their marginal productivity. This assertion does not hold up in law, and it is economically false.

The law does not recognize the enterprise; it only recognizes the private company. The enterprise is a collective entity, a human grouping devoted to the production of social utilities. A human grouping cannot belong to anyone. By contrast, the private company is a legal entity establishing a corporate body that embodies the purpose of the enterprise. It is the private company, and it alone, that makes commitments in the name of the enterprise. Because the private company is a legal entity, it delegates its powers to a governing body – its board of directors – which mandates an executive that is itself hierarchically organized. Nothing in this legal disposition resembles a principal–agent relationship between shareholders and enterprise. The board of directors is not the agent of a principal, but the strategic body of an institution.

The beneficiaries of the private company are all contributors of assets that make it possible for the private company to perform its mission: the accumulation of value. Shareholders contribute a type of asset. That is why they are owners of capital shares in the private company. But other partners in the enterprise contribute different assets, which are essential to its efficacy, even if they are not recognized as property rights in the company. The enterprise is a collective that is effective by virtue of the cooperation and complementarity of its talents. The relations underlying its productive efficacy cannot be assimilated to 'quasi-market' relations. It is therefore illusory to purport to assess each employee's individual marginal contribution to the value produced. Correspondingly, the company's stock-market valuation is not an adequate measure of the social utility created by the enterprise.

The enterprise's productivity results essentially from a collective learning process: tacit knowledge, produced by the circulation of skills, that enhances individual abilities; informal interaction between employees within horizontal structures; the motivation of wage-earners as partners. These sources of productive efficiency are crushed by shareholder governance, which does not recognize the social contract required to enhance them.

The squandering of human resources and the French employment deficit

The enterprise's human stock is a collective asset. Its recognition and appreciation condition development. It is essential to regard it as an investment, not as intermediate consumption. The policies that determine such investment are only effective if they are integrated into corporate strategic planning. There is therefore a chain of intangible value deriving from the dynamic interdependence between individual intangible assets – for example, the role of tacit knowledge resulting from direct contact between participants in a new investment project. The specific value of digital-revolution technologies (virtual platforms) is to bring together formerly dispersed skills.[4] Innovation good-will (quasi-profit) is created by this synergy. Individuals possessing combined skills are stakeholders in profits, and must participate in corporate governance, as they are beneficiaries of the firm's total value.

Robotization and automation are expanding, and new platforms of interconnection are making customer relations more responsive and volatile. The upshot is a shortage of unskilled jobs in industry and a proliferation of fragmented jobs in services. Such disintegration of the employment relationship increasingly clashes with citizens' aspirations.

Only massive investment in skills, based on a right to continuous lifelong training, can create employment in jobs that appeal to creative and social intelligence – hence not casual jobs or jobs liable to be replaced by intelligent machines.[5] Few French enterprises accept these possibilities. That is why casual labour is exploding as the only alternative to unemployment. Temporary work and fixed-term contracts account for at least 70 per cent of recruitment in recent years. This will increase with the job-security legislation that makes collective redundancy easier, and with the termination of contracts that simplifies individual redundancy. These are provisions to safeguard employers in accordance with shareholder governance, by blaming wage-earners for the job shortage that is in reality due to austerity policies. It takes a good deal of cynicism to go on claiming that the French labour market is rigid when temporary work accounts for over 15 per cent of salaried employment.

Let us be clear about what has occurred. The government, company directors and the financial establishment are on the same wavelength. The macro-financial reasons for prolonged stagnation (see Chapter 1) are shrugged off in favour of an explanation according to which the sole reason for French stagnation is the excessive cost of labour. In seeking to replace the employment/unemployment duality with the casual jobs/skilled jobs duality, one turns one's back on inclusive growth. One also turns one's back on growth *tout court*. For this policy has an insidious, deleterious, long-term impact on productivity. On the one hand, the economy specializes in low-productivity service sectors with little potential for innovation. On the other, the incentive for lifelong investment in human resources diminishes. This tends to damage progress in productivity.

As has recently been shown by Xerfi, France lacks jobs at all levels of the labour market because the jobs on offer do not match the skills of those seeking work.[6] At all levels, applicants must accept jobs that are downgraded in relation to their skills. A downgrading domino effect ensues, projecting unemployment onto the least skilled, creating the illusion that the problem derives from excessive wages at the bottom of the scale. But the outcome is a gigantic squandering of human resources in the whole economy.

The System of Innovation and Competitiveness: The French Desert

Technological progress essentially derives from the exchange of know-how, which creates an external network between firms. It is a mixture of effects of territorial organization (association between firms to develop advanced research together) and informal exchanges. How do these effects external to firms improve the overall productivity of their productive resources? Because the productivity of the intangible capital (human resources, knowledge) of each firm in the network is increased thanks to the technological progress generated by their participation in innovation projects conducted in common by the group of firms in the network.

The creation and operation of such networks of innovation are never spontaneous. They do not proceed from the market, though obviously ultimate market exploitation of the innovations that flow from them is their underlying incentive. A conducive organization is required – a multiform social process in which we can distinguish three main components. First, there are fiscal incentives for enterprise creation, but this is not the most important factor. Second, there is close cooperation between innovative firms – often SMEs and ISEs – and university research laboratories, or the R&D laboratories of big firms. The case of Japan is exemplary in this respect. Rather than shamelessly exploiting their subcontractors, major Japanese enterprises include them in their technological development set-up, guaranteeing them stable finance and cooperation with their own researchers and technicians in a framework of jointly developed projects. Third, there are forms of financing in capital reserves, varying greatly depending on the systems of innovation, so that the SMEs involved are not unduly exposed to debt.

Thus, competitiveness based on intangible capital, and integrating industry and services, extends the enterprise's stakeholders beyond the legal boundaries of the private company. Intangible assets, being effective by virtue of their collective organization, do not have clearly defined property rights. They are sources of positive externalities between the enterprise, other enterprises, public entities, and communities of citizens in the areas where the enterprises are based. They connect industry and services, corporate strategies and economic policies, in such a way that market supply becomes involved in societal issues: the energy transition, the circular economy, urban renewal, health and lifestyles. To take advantage of this coordination, a form of governance is needed that acknowledges the diversity, capacity for interaction and mobility of human skills – hence, extended partnership governance.

There is no dominant system of innovation. Each system is distinguished by the cultural traditions of civil societies, the philosophies of education and ideologies that shape corporate outlooks. We are familiar with the innovation system of venture capital, which prevails in the United States. Individualism is preponderant there in the spirit of enterprise. Budding entrepreneurs, often hailing from public research laboratories, enjoy the aid of 'business angels' who launch them on a development path in innovation zones where entrepreneurs are closely interdependent. Expansion is pursued thanks to investment capital funds that avoid premature dependency on debt. NASDAQ is the judge of success or failure. Success takes the form either of absorption into a large enterprise or conversion into an autonomous public limited company.

This approach to industrial organization is far removed from Asian traditions. Japan closely integrates SMEs into the value chains of large firms, as noted above. China's *guanxi* capitalism is moulded in solidarity networks that are strongly rooted in Confucian tradition. Extended family relations, bonds of trust based on mutual services and shared ethical norms are cements that persist over time.

The absence of a distinctive innovation system in France compared with the German Mittelstand

During the Trente Glorieuses postwar golden age, France constructed an efficient industrial system organized by the state – what might be called an 'industrial-state system of innovation'. Public enterprises were its spearhead. Aeronautics, land transport, the nuclear industry and chemicals were sectors of industrial integration. The state directly dominated finance with the aid of the Caisse des Dépôts et Consignations (CDC). The state's retreat, and the political conversion to market fundamentalism in the 1980s, and especially the 1990s, left the country without a strategy for industrial conversion in the context of global competition.

The fuzziness of French industrial organization contrasts with the *Mittelstand*, which is the benchmark for competitive excellence in Europe. The reinforcement of Germany's exporting power since the creation of the euro forms a pair with the gradual deindustrialization of France. German enterprises have invested massively in eastern Europe to increase the competitiveness of innovation systems on their soil. They have integrated their investment abroad in industrial systems established in the *Länder*. By contrast, under the influence of their Anglo-American shareholders, French enterprises have detached themselves from home territory, even de-territorializing research centres.

The *Mittelstand* is a kind of self-reproduced ecosystem, creating a virtuous circle upon which its resilience to shocks and historical longevity depend.[7] The heart of the system is the quality of intangible assets, which is renewed over time. It makes possible continuous incremental innovation – what is called 'perfection of the ordinary'. It is therefore not a system that makes dazzling breakthroughs with radical innovations. But this incremental innovation, diffused throughout industry, feeds non-price competitive advantages that ensure solid market shares compatible with high margins. Thanks to the solidity of trading accounts, self-financing is the primary source of investment. This encourages independence from finance, and hence continuity in capitalist control by primarily family shareholders. The maintenance of such control enables supervisory boards, on which wage-earners enjoy equal representation, to assert their strategic independence into the distant future, and to negotiate external finance from a position of strength. This is the crucial condition for finance to be placed in the service of the economy. Thanks to this independence, specialization strategies can be pursued that maintain incremental innovation and hence market shares.

The lessons of the German experience

Three lessons can be drawn from the German experience. In the first place, innovation is most often incremental, starting from a controlled industrial base. Second, small niches at a national level can yield highly profitable exports to global markets. Third, a vast range of activities can be protected from the competition of emerging countries if one can innovate in one's specialisms.

Social innovation is the predominant factor in competitiveness: public efforts to train and retrain workers, and a close link between enterprises and educational institutions in the learning process. To this must be added what Germany lacks, but Scandinavia possesses: gender equality in employment and professional mobility and public support for pre-school child-care.

The self-sustaining dynamic of industrial growth involves organizing the relations between public power and private actors. It also requires policies devoted to innovation systems. Industrial strategy must be embedded in local areas. In France, it is down to the regions to promote a new mentality.[8] They must select enterprises capable of developing regional competitive advantages, identify promising segments of industries, and embark on joint pilot projects with public–private co-financing.

To encourage SMEs to innovate and export, it might be useful to introduce in France the status of innovative SME, which would grant access to attractive finance, and to help SMEs abroad much more effectively. Finally, the tasks of re-territorializing industry and creating streams of incremental innovation rest on defining sustainable development as the axis of a strategy at once European and national. This issue will be examined in Chapter 9.

5.

How Should European
Finance be Reorganized?

In Chapters 1–4, I tried to take stock of the eurozone, paying particular attention to France. To do this, I have conjugated several dimensions – macroeconomic, institutional and structural – of what is commonly called the European project. The upshot is Europe's economic impairment and political inability to meet the challenge posed by the incompletion of the euro.

Not that nothing has been done; Chapter 2 described the institutional responses ventured in the course of the crisis. But political initiative has not gone beyond intergovernmental coordination. Without democratic sovereignty at the currency level, intergovernmental steering cannot define the common good from a long-term perspective. Trapped in the network of their reciprocal constraints, states have partly convergent and partly contradictory interests. The only method open to this mode of governance is negotiating compromises out of citizens' sight and beyond their understanding. Since they do not fundamentally resolve the problems, such compromises are temporary and fragile. However, institutional advances since 2010, described in detail in Chapter 2, have given them a certain continuity and irreversibility.

Taking these results as a point of departure, in the following chapters I will seek answers to the problems I have identified by proposing an endogenous institutional dynamic, in the belief that the gravest danger confronting the European project is the threat of secular stagnation. Granted that restoring growth and converting it into inclusive, sustainable growth are the goals that will enable the European project to advance, we must identify the feasible forms of institutional advance indispensable to achieving these goals in the various areas where regulatory deficits have emerged. The idea is that partial institutional advances contain forms of cooperation at EU level, and transfers of power to it, which will eventually win acceptance of the need for an original type of political sovereignty – an imbricated hierarchy allocating supreme political authority to Europe in areas where coordination and unification are most effective, and supreme authority to nation-states in other areas. This kind of double democracy[1] would be distinguished from national federation in that it would entail no encompassing sovereignty, since the monopoly on legitimate violence – the source of real power – would rest with states.

The first area where institutional change is urgent is unquestionably finance. That is why the principle of banking union was finally adopted. Completing banking union is the main concern, but is far from sufficient. Two further changes are indispensable. First of all, relations between currency and finance must change so that monetary policy is concerned with financial stability as a constant objective. This involves altering the remit of the European Central Bank (ECB) as defined in the Maastricht Treaty. Next, the

European financial system must be rebalanced by reducing the undue importance of banks in credit, and innovations must be made to construct financial intermediation capable of financing the long term.

Completing Banking Union and Developing the Banking Model

In Chapter 2, it was pointed out that banking union has become unavoidable, even for political leaders once ferociously hostile to it. Systemic banking crises affect potential growth because they result from a prolonged accumulation of weaknesses in balance sheets. In Europe, these weaknesses have created vicious circles, producing government debt and fragmentation of the European financial area. The priority is to break the spiral between a paralyzed banking system and depressed economic activity. Banking union is thus indispensable to recovering a capacity for financial intermediation.

The handicap of a still-ailing banking system is evident in the fact that major borrowers (non-financial large enterprises and financial institutions) are deserting banks because they find better borrowing terms in the markets. At the same time, other borrowers are suffering very tight credit conditions. Finally, according to the Bank for International Settlements (BIS), the market value of numerous European banks is still below their book value, reflecting market scepticism as to whether balance sheets describe the true financial situation.[2]

The rationale for scepticism lies in the fact that the evaluation of asset quality and the performance of serious stress tests have been delayed for several years. The ability of the banks' capital to absorb future losses is all the weaker because of the amount of unacknowledged losses on assets inherited from the past. In a way, what is dead maintains its grip over what is living. This is most evident in the Italian banking system. These losses increase over time because, in order not to acknowledge them, banks have to continue to support insolvent borrowers by renewing their loans on a larger scale as their losses increase. That is why, according to the BIS, the proportions of bad loans by Spanish and Italian banks continued to grow six years after the paroxysm of the crisis, to beyond 10 per cent, and even 12.5 per cent, of total lending. Relatedly, according to the ECB, around 16 per cent of applications for loans by SMEs were rejected in Italy and Spain in 2013, compared with 11 per cent in 2011. In France, the percentage rose from 9 per cent in 2011 to 13 per cent in 2013, whereas it was reduced by two-thirds in Germany, from 6 per cent in 2011 to 2 per cent in 2013.

So as to keep banks that do not function properly in business, the ECB had to deluge them with unlimited liquidity at practically zero interest rates, which the banks used to purchase the government bonds of solvent states. The banks thus manufactured profit margins without risk. This mechanism encouraged the status quo – national supervisory authorities' negligence when it comes to the state of bank balance sheets – resulting in the large-scale poor allocation of savings, reflected in the continuous fall in productive investment.

Thus we can see that banking union is a crucial step towards completing the euro, as the weaknesses in the banking system imperil the unity of the currency itself. A currency must be unitary in its sphere of circulation. All forms of currency must be fungible – fully convertible into one another – wherever issued and whatever the form in which they are held. Member countries of the eurozone have very different systems for guaranteeing deposits and very different capacities for performing their role, as a result of the poor fiscal situation of weak countries. As long as deposit guarantees are not unified and weak banks are not restructured, it is far from clear that all demand deposits in euros are equal. That is why the three prudential pillars of currency unity must be unified at eurozone level: bank supervision, resolution of bank failures, deposit guarantees. This triptych is supposed to apply to banks that are 'too big to fail' – too large and interconnected to be allowed to collapse.

The achievement of banking union: a laborious process

Banking union is effected in stages. A single mechanism of supervision by the ECB is currently operative, with an assessment of asset quality and then stress tests for the 130 banks that were said to be systemic during 2014, covering the eurozone and most other EU countries. On the other hand, the single resolution mechanism has not yet taken definitive shape, on account of differences of view between governments and tensions between the Council and the European Parliament. Finally, deposit guarantees have been set to one side.

The ECB's extended competence allows for general supervision of the risks of cross-border banks, instead of illusory cooperation between national supervisors, especially in that it has the power to impose its criteria on the national supervisors of banks it does not directly control. Following the stress tests, banks with insufficient capital reserves will be made public, and will be obliged to recapitalize. Those that cannot, either with their own resources or by recourse to the market, will be placed under the responsibility of the resolution authority. But it is the ECB, following its diagnosis, that will determine whether a bank should be subject to the resolution process with the approval of the Resolution Board – which can, however, override reluctance on the ECB's part.

The Single Resolution Mechanism (SRM) is crucial, because it is an institutional device for averting the serial propagation of bank failures. But here we once again encounter ambiguities in transfers of power via institutional changes in the context of inter-state governance; states wish to retain a firm grip on the process through suspected compromises on the Resolution Board. A Single Resolution Fund will be created from 2015 and subscribed to by contributions from banks. It will take eight years for it to reach its balance level of €55 billion! What will happen before then, and particularly at the end of the acid test conducted by the ECB? Furthermore, it seems decidedly small for a systemic crisis, especially given that no joint public guarantee from the Fund has thus far been foreseen in the event of exhaustion of its resources (a backstop), even if the resolution rules must first appeal to the banks' private creditors (bail-in), to asset transfers in hive-offs that remain national, or to liquidation of the bank.

It is clear that an effective banking union would have to contain a federal and independent resolution agency, like the ECB in the area of supervision. Resistance to this betrays the real ambiguity of European decision-making, which haltingly constructs federal institutions through a political apparatus within which final decisions remain intergovernmental.

In the short term, at any rate – that is, with the issue of the ECB's diagnosis in autumn 2014 – resolution will remain national. That is why a critical period is going to begin, which might see a resurgence in market anxieties about sovereign debt, if states with weak finances are required to recapitalize systemic banks whose audit has revealed vulnerability. The European Stability Mechanism (ESM) will have to be mobilized to re-float some banks. The ESM has the power to recapitalize banks directly to the tune of €60 billion, on condition of unanimity among member countries.

The Terra Nova think tank proposes an alternative temporary solution of solidarity before the permanent apparatus of the Resolution Fund becomes fully operational.[3] The systemic banks that might pose the biggest problems are always transnational – that is, they have branches and subsidiaries in several countries. It is therefore logical for all the countries that host these banks' activities to contribute to their resolution where necessary, and not only the country where the parent company's headquarters are sited. Member countries could thus agree on a rule of loss-sharing a priori, so that the residual losses to be covered by a bank in resolution, after absorption by the bail-in, are not a burden exclusively on the weak country that is home to the bank's headquarters.

Banking union and the role of banks in financing the economy

The financial crisis calls into question polarized models for financing economies: on the one hand, the all-market Wall Street model, intermediated by international investment banks that are financed in a wholesale liquidity market with enormous leverage; on the other, the European model of universal banks whose share in financing the economy is predominant. The Liikanen Report for the European Commission demonstrated that the size of these banking monsters was utterly excessive in relation to the economies that are home to them: the total assets of Deutsche Bank are 80 per cent of German GDP, those of HSBC 120 per cent of British GDP, those of BNP Paribas 100 per cent of French GDP, and so on.

According to the BIS, the all-purpose bank is in the process of going out of fashion in the Anglo-American model.[4] Three specialist banking models can be distinguished. The first, which is becoming fashionable because it is the most profitable and robust, is the retail banking model, which offers straightforward loans, has a stable income, and possesses a regular source of finance via deposits. The second is the investment bank model, which provides for corporations' external growth operations, restructuring and complex projects, and which borrows on the wholesale liquidity market. The third is the arbitrage bank model, which is active in securities transactions and financed in the inter-banking market and through issues of market debt. This model is in retreat on account of its operating costs, swollen as they are by the extravagant remuneration of analysts and managers and new supervisory rules extended to off-balance-sheet items.

In Europe, specialization might derive from the banking resolution rules that oblige banks to prepare plans for their possible breakup. This should provide an incentive to distinguish types of business and concentrate them in separate subsidiaries. This development is more likely in that the European Parliament is determined to reform bank structures in line with the Liikanen Report. Bank structures must therefore be developed in the direction of a clear distinction between types of banking model. Finally, the undue influence of banks in Europe must be reduced. This implies a different model of long-term finance and investment, which will be discussed in the third section of this chapter.

The separation into autonomous subsidiaries imposed on the banks is all the more necessary to give effect to a rule of loss-sharing, in that cross-border banks seek to do the opposite. They treat their subsidiaries as branches intrinsically linked to the parent company in cases of resolution. The more opaque and integrated the structure of a bank in resolution, the more conflict-resolution will involve when it comes to sharing out the cost between countries. With separation, both supervision and resolution will become more transparent.

These arrangements are important for improving the strength of banks; but they do not radically alter the mentality of bankers. Since the start of the wave of deregulation and expansion of financial markets in the 1980s, the banking model has been based on the preponderance of debt leverage over bank liabilities, on the pretext that capital reserves are expensive, and consequently interfere with loans on the asset side. Vulnerability derives principally from the microeconomic behaviour of bankers, prompted by the guarantee enjoyed by banks because they create money. A relationship is established between options on the asset side and the composition of liabilities. How can such a relationship exist?

A major work has recently supplied the theoretical basis for understanding this anomaly and justifying the proposal to compel banks to hold far greater capital reserves (20–30 per cent of the balance sheet) than is advocated by the regulation of Basel III.[5] In conditions of market efficiency, hence perfect competition, the total value of bank assets assessed at market prices is equal to the total value of liabilities – that is, the total value of debts and capital reserves. This means that the social return on bank investments is equal to the total social cost of the commitments that finance them, without the ratio between capital reserves and debts being taken into account.[6] Since things are never thus, there are distortions that create inefficiency in finance. The upshot of these distortions is that bankers do not pay the social cost of financing their operations. This is what makes banks special, and why they must be subject to special regulation. Conversely, to believe in the efficiency of finance is not only to believe that markets are perfectly competitive, but also to believe in finance without money!

Since the market economy is monetary, demand for money by economic agents is an inescapable reality. Since banks are the main issuers of money, they necessarily have a debt in their liabilities, because banking deposits are the main component of money. But money is a public good. Its efficacy lies in the fact that all its components must be fungible, and hence fully equivalent. It follows that deposits must be protected on pain of systemic crisis. This socializes the cost of their protection through the function of the government as lender of last resort. Consequently, banks do not pay for the social cost of financing their loans. In these circumstances, their debt is less costly for them than their capital reserves. With the development of financial innovations – above all credit derivatives and securitization of loans, which enable banks to shuffle off the risks of their lending onto other actors – moral hazard knows no limits. In pushing debt leverage to absurd levels, the international banking lobby deliberately created uncontrolled exposure to risk, and plunged the world economy into systemic crisis.

Regulation must therefore be in a position to counter the fact that banks are not exposed to the full risk entailed in their decisions. Admati and Hellwig's recommendation is to select a ratio of capital to total assets on the non-weighted balance sheet. In fact, the weighted ratios that allow banks to manipulate the denominator at will need to be abolished. This ratio should give effect to the following compromise: it must be sufficiently high for the probability of bank failure to be negligible, but sufficiently low not to impede demand for bank money by economic agents; if the proportion of capital reserves in the balance sheet is too high, banks will not be able to respond flexibly to demand for money. According to the authors, this ratio of capital reserves to the total balance sheet would be of the order of 20–30 per cent.

The Requisite *Aggiornamento* of Monetary Policy

Prior to the financial crisis, monetary policy in the euro-zone corresponded to a 'monetarist' outlook. This formed part of an ideological movement that became dominant in the late 1970s in the fight against the generalized inflation of these years. At the same time, financial deregulation and globalization completely altered the way that finance had been managed in the previous thirty years.

Monetarism's main idea is the neutrality of money. This is tantamount to hypothesizing finance without money – hence efficient in the sense that the social return on real investment is independent of the composition of the forms of saving that finance it. Essentially, if money is properly managed, and hence neutral in this conception, it has no effect on the real economy, or the overall level of economic activity, or the allocation of production between categories of goods and of incomes between economic agents. All the central bank has to do is ensure price stability – more precisely, anchor the medium-term expectations of economic agents to a modest stated inflation rate of the order of 2 per cent per annum. To achieve this, it must regularly alter the mass of money by manipulating its key rate. Because finance is assumed to be 'efficient', this interest rate suffices to guide the whole structure of credit and asset prices in such a way that expanding the mass of money is compatible with the inflation target. Hence the prevailing slogan until the crisis: 'one objective (inflation rate), one tool (key interest rate)'. This epoch had a splendid name – the 'Great Moderation' – even as financial imbalances were accumulating at top speed!

In Europe, the doctrine was perfectly in accord with the spirit of Maastricht, because it was compatible with the euro's incompletion. The ECB, being the sole federal institution in a non-federal monetary area, was to have unparalleled independence. Not only did the ECB, like its counterparts, have independent means, but it had independent objectives. It decreed the inflation target it was obliged to meet! The neutrality of money is thus a crucial credo, for, without it, monetary policy has powerful redistributive effects. And that is precisely what happened, as we saw at the start of Chapter 3 (Figure 3.1). It follows that its statutes, which are completely de-territorialized, authorize the ECB to make social choices implicitly, outside any democratic control.

It is supposed not to have any relationship with any state and hence, above all, not to purchase government debt securities in secondary government bond markets. This would lead it into explicit, as opposed to implicit, choices. Yet, to abstain from doing something is as much a choice as doing it – unless, obviously, it is assumed that doing or not doing has the same effect! And an outright turn to the hypothesis of the neutrality of money has been made. This allows the ECB not to be accountable to any sovereign institution, be it governments or parliaments. Courtesy sessions, where the president of the ECB appears before the European Parliament, have nothing to do with retrospective control of the Central Bank by the sovereign institution that is the guarantor of its statutes. The ECB fixes its own inflation target and controls itself. In short, 'it is at the window and watches itself passing in the street'. All this until the financial crisis!

We saw in Chapter 1 that the financial crisis was not a bolt from the blue. It was the fork in the road where large-scale, long-term imbalances that had accumulated in the financial cycle were transformed into a phase of contraction called balance-sheet deflation. This means that finance is not what is claimed by the theory of efficiency that justifies monetarism. Consequently, the monetary policy advocated by the slogan 'one objective, one tool' is untenable. Chapter 2 showed how central banks reacted pragmatically in the crisis. This also applies to the ECB. But it is handicapped by the euro's incompletion, which continues to prevent it from acting on finance by buying government debt.

At all events, the question that concerns us now is this: What of the post-crisis? Since banking union is underway, and the ECB has a key role in it as supervisor, are the information and warning signals received in this position going to affect monetary policy? More fundamentally, with finance having proved its inability to regulate itself, and with the monetarist hypothesis that no major crisis can occur if inflation is contained having been so dramatically falsified, it seems inconceivable that monetary policy could return to its errant ways. Since systemic risk is in the grip of radical uncertainty, money and finance cannot be separated.

Crisis pragmatism must be converted into a doctrine that incorporates financial stability as a fully fledged objective of monetary policy. But how is this objective to be expressed? What are the tools for achieving it? How is it connected to the inflation target? In addition, government debt securities are the pivot of the whole structure of financial assets. Can a policy of financial stability be implemented while continuing to ignore government debt? These are the questions that must be answered in order to renew the doctrine of monetary policy.

A new dimension for monetary policy:
macro-prudential purpose

Recurrent financial crises derive from cumulative excesses in credit expansion, and an increase in asset prices disconnected from the real conditions of productivity that determine capital profitability. These excesses obey a logic of momentum, where the upward movement is maintained by the dynamic interdependence of financial actors. To interact with such processes in order to contain them, central banks must understand their deep causes. These stand in contrast to what is taught by the orthodox theory of finance, for which strategic interaction between financial actors is irrelevant. In effect, each actor is supposed to have complete information about the determinants of asset valuation and to have a psychological attitude to risk independent of market conditions.

We must therefore change paradigms and accept the uncertainty hypothesis. In an uncertain universe, the time of the future and the time of the past are not uniform. It is therefore not possible to delimit the set of contingent events and assign them objective laws of probability that are common to them all. Relatedly, faced with an uncertain future, attitudes to risk can no longer be regarded as an exogenous psychological feature. Hence the possibility of momentum, which feeds off increasingly high debt leverage.

In positive terms, a different hypothesis must be developed, which accepts the endogenous character of attitudes to risk, incorporated in the price of risk. Keynes stressed this point: the stamp of uncertainty in individual behaviour. The price of risk varies with the scale of asset price volatility, generating a powerfully nonlinear dynamic. In the euphoric phase of the rise in asset markets, volatility is low and the appetite for risk increases, reinforcing enthusiasm for the rise. By contrast, the bifurcation of the downturn increases uncertainty, because its timing is radically uncertain. Attitudes to risk become more hesitant, distrustful and cautious, while volatility grows. Greater uncertainty smothers momentum. Any market mishap or hint that monetary policy might change is enough to cause panic, setting off a cascade of sales orders.

The dilemma of finance is thus as follows: the lower the price of risk incorporated in the returns on assets, the more vulnerable finance is to systemic risk. This dilemma comprises an interaction between micro- and macroeconomic levels that is opposed to the 'orthodox' theory. Coordination via the future creates collective attitudes to risk that range from euphoria to stress and panic: risk is overvalued and becomes systemic in crises because it has been undervalued in prior episodes of collective euphoria.

It is illuminating to turn to a stylized representation of the relations between price of risk and financial vulnerability.[7] Let us call the price of risk p, financial shocks s, and the degree of vulnerability of the financial system V. Shocks occur and intensify in the downturn of the financial cycle. According to the theory of financial instability, p is a function of s and V. It is an increasing, convex function of s, and the more convex in that vulnerability is high when shocks are powerful. This applies when the leverage momentum has fuelled a large speculative bubble. By contrast, when shocks are minor at the start of the phase of financial expansion, the risk price paid by market participants, p, is lower in as much as latent but concealed vulnerability is high. The sensitivity of the price of risk to financial shocks is therefore expressed by the curve of the function V. A more prudent financial organization (V') will induce financial intermediaries to display greater caution when shocks are minor, but that will make it possible to control the risk price better when shocks are sizeable (the curve of the function V' is less pronounced than that of the function V). Hence the dilemma of monetary policy depicted in the graph below: a policy that encourages a significant decrease in the price of risk, because inflation is low, results in vulnerability that will cause the price of risk to jump subsequently.

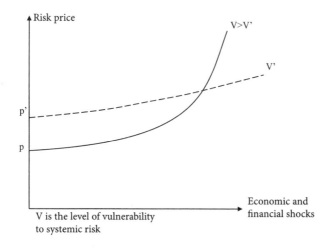

Risk price

V>V'

V'

p'

p

Economic and financial shocks

V is the level of vulnerability to systemic risk

To prevent central banks being forced into ex-post rescues, whose scale and duration cannot be controlled, macro-prudential policy is a new tool dedicated to the stability of the financial system as a whole. In a sense, it is intermediate between traditional supervisory regulation and monetary policy. To achieve its objective, macro-prudential policy must maintain the price of risk at a sufficiently high level in the phase of financial expansion to avoid its rising in a destructive fashion during the downturn. This involves influencing the arbitrage price of the risk/probability of systemic crisis, inherent in the intrinsic instability of finance. To alter the conditions of this arbitrage, it is necessary to act on underlying, structural and dynamic weaknesses.

Structural weaknesses derive from the interconnections and complexities of market intermediation. They are forms of risk exposed to the coordination defects that are cradles of systemic risk. They result from opaque series of counterparty risks in the mutual transfers of risk that sustain the explosion in asset growth. They also flow from the liquidity risk attributable to the financing of intermediaries in a liquidity wholesale market that might be paralyzed under the impact of stress, as in September–October 2008.

Dynamic weaknesses are endogenous to the financial cycle. They are the growing leverage of intermediaries bound up with the momentum in asset prices and increasing mismatches in maturity through recourse to the market in ever shorter debt to finance long, non-liquid assets.

The conduct of monetary policy must take account of the whole configuration of risks involved in macro-prudential regulation, because it varies in the financial cycle with dynamic weaknesses. The two types of policy – macro-prudential and monetary – are therefore linked. But their coordination is not self-evident. The reaction time of macro-prudential policy is longer, and the transmission channels less well-known, than those of monetary policy. In addition, continuous diagnosis of the varying probability of a systemic crisis when the financial cycle develops is not a simple matter. To reduce cyclical weaknesses, it must be possible to monitor the variation in the price of risk that flows from strategic interaction between lenders and borrowers. The operational method is macroeconomic stress tests, which have to be carried out periodically. They are performed by the central bank, in conjunction with banks deemed to be of systemic importance on the basis of a list of criteria determined by the central bank. The latter defines the macroeconomic parameters of an extreme scenario in which banks might make losses on their loans and market assets. In addition, the systemic character derives from the fact that the banks have more or less complex cross-loan relations. The central bank communicates the details of the macroeconomic scenario to the banks, and asks them to calculate its impact on their balance sheet and confirm whether they have the required capital reserves to cover such potential losses. The banks' results are communicated to the central bank and cross-checked by experts in banking supervision. Thus the central bank has an overview of structural weaknesses in the banking system. Because performing these tests is onerous, the central bank uses market indicators to track dynamic weaknesses on a day-to-day basis.

As to the macro-prudential tools that have macroeconomic effects, and can therefore be incorporated into monetary policy, there are many of them. Let us cite the requirement of capital buffers, required reserve ratios, loan-to-value ratios, and debt-to-income ratios. Capital ratios modulated over the financial cycle must not rise in the upturn either too soon or too late – hence the need for the use of these tools to be linked up with information furnished by the stress tests. They must fall after the downturn in the cycle, to maintain the flow of lending by banks to the economy when losses materialize in the banking system. However, the effect could be asymmetrical: a modest impact to check the momentum of lending, since the attraction of leverage in the upturn of the financial cycle is strong, but a dampening of credit-rationing in the downturn thanks to the mobilization of reserves that have been built up. The macro-prudential tool could thus relieve central banks, which would have less need to implement ultra-expansionary monetary policies in the crisis.

Financial stability and government debt: a multi-objective monetary policy

The dogma that monetary policy must be independent of fiscal policy makes no sense in the financial cycle. The cycle is generated by private debt, as Chapter 1 made clear. After the downturn in asset prices, periods of debt reduction in the private sector are initially accompanied by a rise in public-sector debt. The fundamental issue in fiscal policy is the pace of government debt reduction contingent on the pace of private debt reduction.[8]

Let us note here that, in the ascending phase of the financial cycle, fiscal policy must be modulated in line with the pace of private-sector debt reduction to enable the central bank to offer an effective counter to a dangerous decline in the inflation rate. This becomes very difficult when nominal interest rates are already close to zero.

Monetary policy and fiscal policy must be coordinated. Less pronounced government debt reduction today makes more sustained private debt reduction possible. This will give fiscal policy room for manoeuvre in the future, ensuring the long-term sustainability of government debt. By reducing the scale of the financial cycle, if it is effective, macro-prudential policy also helps because it reduces the size of the government debt needed during the downturn.

It follows that monetary policy is located at the intersection of three objectives: stability in the general price level (hence in the value of money); financial stability; and sustainability of government debt. The theory of political economy teaches that it is possible to overcome conflicts between objectives if the authority responsible for macroeconomic regulation possesses at least as many tools as objectives. Moreover, these tools must be assigned to the tasks for which they are relatively most effective (see Table 5.1).

Table 5.1: Monetary Policy: Assignment of Tools to Objectives

Objectives	Imbalances to be Controlled	Tools
Price stability	Inflationary spiral/ Phillips Curve	Short-term interest rates
Financial stability	*Momentum:* duration and scale	Macro-prudential tools
Sustainability of government debt	Non-convergent trajectory of debt ratio/GDP	Central bank balance sheet influencing long-term rates

The redefinition of monetary policy leads on to a redefinition of the ECB's remit. The three interdependent objectives cannot be pursued in the interests of the common good without a dialogue between the authorities responsible for economic policy. It follows that Central Bank independence cannot be conceived dogmatically. The inconsistency between the need for an expanded monetary policy and incompletion of the euro is quite evident.

Financing the Long Term

In Chapters 3 and 4, we saw that Europe lags far behind in investment, whether private or public, in physical capital or human resources. The result is a reduction in the rate of technological progress and in the quality of factors of production. People cannot invest in the absence of prospects for growth, and hence without a sufficiently extended horizon to make investment plans and finance them. This is the starting-point for escaping the trap of secular stagnation.

Such prospects involve macroeconomic policy in the first instance. Hence the importance of the articulation of monetary with fiscal policy to which I have just referred. But they also assume a financial system in a position to take long-term risks. In the long run, public investment and private investment are complementary. Public investment nurtures the productivity of private investment. It is therefore indispensable for Europe to direct public expenditure towards investment in infrastructure and human capital, so as to restore the potential growth on which a reduction in structural unemployment depends.

As was noted in Chapter 4, a new conception of industrial policy is necessary. It involves financing both private and public investment, SMEs and the structural networks of innovation systems. There is no shortage of savings to finance such investment. What is lacking is an effective financial system to expand horizons and share risks.

We must draw the lessons from the failure of the model dominated by the international investment bank lobby, which advocates unlimited expansion of debt on the basis of an unregulated wholesale liquidity market. Finally, we must be rid of the illusion that the European model of all-purpose banks can resume normal service to resolve the dilemma of the exigencies of financial stability or the requirement of massive investment. Finally, asset-valuation and risk-sharing must be conceived differently. This requires different actors and a different conception of financial intermediation.

Three directions seem promising: removing the obstacles facing financial actors who are potentially long-term investors, but who are incentivized not to be; creating channels and instruments of non-banking finance adapted to the life-cycle of enterprises; and organizing collaboration between public and private financial actors for a new financial intermediation on a European scale.

Adapting prudential regulation and accounting norms to long-term investors

There are two types of long-term investor. On the one hand, pension funds with a defined benefit regime and life insurance companies are financial actors that have liability commitments involving providing savers with guaranteed incomes for fixed terms. Their overriding objective is immunization of their liabilities, which is itself long term. On the other hand, state development banks and sovereign funds, whose liabilities are state capital funds, have objectives involving the investment of public resources that are not subject to fiscal rules and which do not have any contractual framework either. But they are in the service of the nation, through parliamentary or government control depending on the nature of the political regime.

The investment horizon of most of these actors is, in principle, sufficiently extended to internalize the financial cycle. They can therefore avoid the logic of momentum. However, in financial environments disrupted by the excesses of market finance, these investors have not conducted themselves in accordance with the paradigm of long-term finance. There is therefore a potential for untapped saving that risks being further aggravated by future regulations. It is therefore better to adapt the new regulations to the nature of investors' liabilities.

This is the case with life insurance companies subject to the prudential framework of Solvency II, which strengthens solvency requirements, and to asset accountancy in terms of market value, which is going to introduce short-term asset volatility into their balance sheets. These two constraints will lead insurance companies to reduce their exposure to risk so as to reduce capital outlay.

Pension funds are not subject to prudential norms, but to two main forms of regulation:[9] standards of prudence and quantitative limits on investment, depending on the class of assets. The prudential rule is more flexible, as it seeks to minimize the overall risk of the portfolio. For their part, accounting norms in market value require recognition of all balance-sheet surpluses and deficits in real time. They therefore aim to return the volatility of financial markets to the level of the measurement of retirement benefits, which encourages a decrease in risk-taking.

Sovereign wealth funds have no contractual commitments. They therefore have the potential to invest in the class of assets of their choice. However, freedom of investment is strictly monitored by the central bank or economics ministry. Consequently, they have been managed rather conservatively.

Prudential and accountancy norms ignore the specific characteristics of long-term investment, thus making sources of long-term finance scarcer. Consequently, such regulation should be altered to adapt the diversity of financial actors to different economic models, and avoid destabilizing effects from short-termist mimetic behaviour. This can be done by treating these investors' assets in line with the quality and stability of their liabilities. As to asset valuation, a long-term view involves accepting smoothing mechanisms. For these categories of investor, anything that encourages pro-cyclical asset management should be discouraged: benchmark management, termly reporting, recourse to ratings agencies, index-linking managerial pay to short-term returns – everything that delights asset management seeking to corner capital gains amid market volatility. Non-banking finance cannot be strong if investors who are large contributors of savings do not take responsibility for controlling their credit risks. Accountancy norms should also be revised: mark-to-market accountancy should be abolished in favour of securities that retain their long-term value, provided they are not subject to short-term selling pressure.

Creating new channels and new instruments of finance adapted to the life-cycle of enterprises

An issue of the first importance is increasing the number of innovative enterprises, and the likelihood that they will grow until they are listed on the stock market. Finance must therefore be adapted to the life-cycle of enterprises by having the best financial organization at each stage. Such financing must prioritize capital reserves. In Chapter 4, we saw that premature or excessive exposure to debt is the main cause of the difficulties faced by SMEs.

When enterprises are created, and in the first stage of their existence, finance is for start-up purposes. It comprises the contributions of founders and their families, micro-finance and business angels. The number of business angels in France is far too low. In many instances, family capital is not sufficiently committed to protecting the enterprise during a difficult phase.

The second phase – the development of start-ups – greatly depends on management monitoring by experienced indi-viduals who have successfully conducted such business in the past. It also demands a much more sizeable investment in capital reserves than the start-up. This is the sphere of venture capital. These specialist funds might come from pools of individual investors or dedicated funds created by long-term investors as elements of their alternative asset allocation. In this phase, risks are higher. That is why venture capital funds must be large enough to follow at least a dozen projects, so as to overcompensate for enterprises that fail by means of the very high profitability of enterprises that make it to commercialization and enter the phase of very strong growth in demand for their products.

The phase of rapid growth is the one requiring the greatest non-market capital contribution. The latter must make the venture capitalists' profitable exit possible. There are two possible forms of contribution in capital stock at this stage: private investment by asset-management companies and private equity funds (PEs) created by long-term investors. The second, in particular, are essential. Unlike the PEs of the 2000s, which were composed of predatory funds operating essentially through debts on mature enterprises, the PE funds under consideration here are pure investors in capital. The expansion of private equity under the auspices of major non-banking investors will probably be one way of stimulating bottom-up innovation in future years.

Listing on the stock market is the last phase, in which these modes of finance give way to the injection of capital through the stock market for enterprises at cruising speed. This is where long-term investors are of great importance in averting enterprises falling under the sway of shadow banking. This does not prevent these medium-sized establishments also having need of debt. Appropriate techniques must therefore be employed to limit the cost of credit and diversify loans, thanks to debt markets that can contribute a broad spectrum of financial instruments. We may cite asset finance and securitization of long-term debts. To incentivize banks to extend the structured credit beyond the equity tranche, the Central Bank could accept as refinancing collateral 'plain vanilla' – i.e. uniform and standard – ABS (asset-backed securities), whose securitization process would be strictly supervised by the European market regulation authorities.

A new intermediation on a European scale to promote structural investment

We saw in Chapter 1 (Figure 1.2) that public investment has been the first casualty of financialized capitalism since the start of the 1980s. Western societies are eroding the collective basis of social capital. The countries where this has gone furthest are the United States, the United Kingdom and Germany. A recent IMF study has recalled the positive contribution of public investment to short- and long-term growth. The study also stresses that the current period of weak growth, low inflation, rock-bottom interest rates and the persistence of a level of activity below potential is ideal for undertaking an ambitious programme of investment in infrastructure.[10] The new European Commission chaired by Jean-Claude Juncker envisages a €300 billion plan for the whole European Union over three years. This so-called Juncker Plan was re-scaled to €500 billion in 2016. Its content is vague, and it would be financed simply by activating the idle resources of the European budget and European Investment Bank.

The virtues of a European public investment programme

The IMF study ranges far beyond Europe, but it supplies timely arguments for a programme for Europe, which is seriously short of them. The study observes that public capital stock has declined as a proportion of global GDP for more than three decades. In the aforementioned developed economies, infrastructure has aged considerably, and inadequate maintenance affects service quality.

Public investment increases activity in the short term through a demand impact and in the long term through a supply impact. The scale of the demand impact depends on the position in the cycle and on monetary policy. It is enhanced when activity is below the potential of economies and when monetary policy is loose. In other words, current conditions in Europe are ideal! The supply impact depends on the productivity of investments and the way they are financed. It is important for project selection to be geared to securing private investment, aiming for maximum complementarity. Financing must also be adapted to the investment's gestation period, to avoid delays and cost overruns.

If financing is so conceived as not to create additional government debt in the case of highly indebted countries, creating distrust in capital markets, an infrastructural investment programme in Europe, in current conditions of a surfeit of idle savings, may have sufficient growth impact to reduce government debt rather than increasing it.

The efficiency of infrastructural investment – its ability to raise the productivity of the whole economy – is crucial for achieving an enduring recovery in European growth. The infrastructure that generates productivity gains in corporate capital comprises means of transport, intelligent networks of electricity distribution, and the information and communications systems required to spread the digital economy to the core of the productive system: skills training, public R&D, and the conservation and reconstruction of ecosystems. Such investment creates positive externalities, whereby the social return on the project, taking account of all the effects generated, is higher than the private return to the operator of the infrastructure. This investment also has very high fixed costs, while the income derived from its future operation extends over a very long period. That is why means of financing such investment must be adapted to these characteristics.

A financial intermediation mobilizing idle savings

In March 2013, the European Commission published a *Green Paper on Long-Term Financing of the European Economy*. It advocated a pivotal role for institutional investors, the promotion of new instruments of long-term finance to increase supply in financial markets, and arrangements for facilitating access by SMEs to non-banking external finance. To finance public goods of European significance, it is also necessary to coordinate the major state development banks that exist in Europe: Kreditanstalt für Wiederaufbau (KfW) in Germany, Caisse des Dépôts et Consignations (CDC) in France, Cassa Depositi et Prestiti (CDP) in Italy, and the Instituto de Credito Oficial (ICO) in Spain. This coordination could be carried out around a European Investment Fund (EIF), which could itself proceed from a restructuring of the European Investment Bank, which has not hitherto played the role that might have been anticipated.[11]

In line with the approach indicated at the start of this chapter, which consists in creating institutions only to resolve clearly identified problems, the EIF would be a federal fund for financing European public goods, props of sustainable growth. To this end, one can envisage its endowment with capital supplied by the European budget, whose 'competitiveness and growth' role would be boosted. Enjoying the joint guarantee of the countries of the European Union, the fund would have the highest financial rating. This would allow it to issue long-term bonds intended for institutional investors and sovereign funds the world over, equipping it with considerable firepower. It could thus both aid national development banks engaged in domestic policies for renovating the productive system and directly finance investment projects of European significance.

This mode of non-market public–private intermediation would complete the restructuring of European finance, which also includes the completion of banking union, the expansion of the ECB's remit, and diversification in the forms of private sector finance. On this financial basis, capable of restoring the overall investment rate in Europe and thus boosting potential growth, it is possible to conceive of an orderly consolidation of government debt.

6.

How Can Government Finances be Made Sustainable without Stifling the Economy?

Public debt is the oldest form of finance. For thousands of years, it has been combined with state power to pursue war – the principal attribute of sovereignty. Taxing, borrowing and the repudiation of debt form a triptych that runs through the ages. With the development of capitalism, private powers revolted against the state and opposed the repudiation of public debt. A parry to this emerged in the twentieth century in the shape of devaluation via inflation. It took the development of financial globalization from the 1980s to make inflation anathema and impose the major institutional change of central bank independence. But the crisis has made it clear that, in financial crises, states which remain fully sovereign – and hence are not failing states – can always place government debt outside the market to the requisite extent, through the central bank's purchase of government bonds.

As Chapter 2 showed, incompletion of the euro has meant that eurozone states are no longer fully sovereign, without a form of sovereignty having been established at the level of the monetary area. It follows that the government debt of member-states is in an ambiguous position. Theoretically, it is reduced to the status of private debt, like any debt issued in foreign currency. We saw that things are not exactly thus, because the European Central Bank (ECB) has been compelled to take 'unconventional' measures to salvage something. But its actions elicited bitter criticism in Germany.

That is why high levels of government debt are a subject of endless controversy, beloved of the media. The controversy is not always rational, and absurd provisions have been made in the United States. Thus, American legislation fixes a borrowing ceiling for the federal state – something that makes no rational sense. When the fateful limit approaches, the political parties rip each other to shreds to wrest concessions, threatening not to vote to raise the ceiling, thereby paralyzing the functioning of the state. Thus we have the absurd situation of representatives refusing to honour expenditure they have already voted for.

Yet the United States does not have a monopoly on the mania for fixing quantitative limits to government finances. The European Fiscal Stability Treaty (see Chapter 2) is peppered with quantitative constraints of all sorts. The oldest are the best known: government debt must not exceed 60 per cent of GDP and the annual deficit must not exceed 3 per cent of GDP. These limits have obviously been shattered as a result of the turmoil caused by financial actors. They have nevertheless been incessantly reaffirmed as preconditions of sound management of public expenditure. Some economists even believe they have discovered magical numbers: above 90 per cent of GDP, government debt allegedly chokes off growth. This sensational announcement, which caused a great stir, has been seriously challenged, including as regards methods for calculating the threshold.[1] The IMF then took up the issue to determine the effects of a high level of debt.[2]

There is no magic threshold. Like Reinhart and Rogoff's 90 per cent level, the arbitrary limit the EU's Fiscal Stability Treaty seeks to impose, in adopting the Maastricht Treaty's 60 per cent level, is null and void. This means that the level of government debt has no negative effect on potential growth when the debt is sustainable over the long term. The sustainability of government debt will be defined precisely in the second section of this chapter. What counts is the pattern of the debt's evolution, at whatever level. However, high debt levels do tend to increase the conjunctural volatility of economic activity, because governments hesitate to implement active counter-cyclical policies during a recession if debt is already high.

Over and above statistical controversies, we may note that the limit-setting approach is concerned exclusively with gross government debt, and takes no account of state assets or who holds the debt. This is like taking an interest in an enterprise's liabilities without looking at what it has by way of assets. In addition, accounting procedures for government finances makes it possible to post very different results. Thus, Japan's gross public debt in 2012 was 238 per cent according to the IMF, and 206 per cent according to the Japanese Finance Ministry. As for net debt, taking the state's negotiable assets into account, it was 133 per cent. Which is the right figure for assessing the scale of the problem with Japan's public finances?

Considering the gross debt only is tantamount to proceeding as if the state produced nothing of value, as if it had no assets, and thus no balance sheet. As I indicated in Chapter 2, this attitude is absurd. The state produces public goods on which social life depends. Without them, neither society nor the market economy would exist. These public goods create intergenerational solidarity. That is why a public debt must exist. The state can play this role only because, unlike all private actors, it is presumed to be immortal. Government debt does not have to be repaid in the way that private debts do, as it lasts indefinitely. That is why it is preferable to replace the notion of solvency with that of viability, or sustainability. In precise economic terms, government debt is said to be sustainable if its value discounted to infinity is nil. This is the only condition that makes economic sense.

What does this condition tell us about managing government debt? The first lesson is that the consolidation of large government debts is a long-term problem. For it to be possible to declare a debt viable or unviable, its total pattern has to be considered. Rushing to try to reduce debt when exceptional events have caused it to balloon spectacularly is more than likely to have the opposite effect: government debt grows further as a result of restrictive economic policies implemented to reduce it. The second lesson is that, to preserve this long-term perspective in a context of financial turmoil bound up with private debt reduction, government debt must be uncoupled from the fragility of the private actors who hold it. Hence the central bank's role in placing this debt off-market to the required extent.

For the eurozone, this means that consolidating government debt and completing the euro go hand-in-hand. Such is our problematic. I shall first adopt a historical perspective, so as to draw some lessons from the past about what does and does not work when it comes to policies to consolidate government debt.

I will then clarify the theoretical definition of a sustainable path, in conditions where the deviation of government debt from its previous path results from rescuing the financial system, whose systemic collapse has been provoked by its own misdemeanours. Thirdly, I will summarize a simulation conducted to identify sustainable paths in the case of France, whose circumstances in the eurozone are average.

The Lessons of History: How are Consolidation Policies to be Implemented?

These lessons are drawn mainly from two in-depth studies carried out collectively with two teams of researchers for the Institut CDC pour la Recherche in 2011 and 2013.[3] They concern historical episodes of large-scale consolidation of government debt, and cover a wide range of developed countries and different historical eras. The lessons are complemented by cases examined by the OECD's economics department.[4]

The approach is very different from that of Reinhart and Rogoff. It does not involve assembling the maximum number of countries and examining only the quantitative relationship between two variables: the gross government debt-to-GDP ratio and GDP growth rate. Instead, it involves studying policies in a large group of countries, and in different eras, aimed at reducing the burden of government debt, starting from the situations that gave rise to it. Comparison on the basis of these experiences seeks to define the conditions for success, or the reasons for failure, of attempts at consolidation.

It is important to distinguish between two types of situation: on the one hand, consolidation motivated by fiscal deterioration caused by previous policies on expenditures or receipts resulting in cumulative deficits, in macroeconomic contexts that might be mediocre, because they follow recessions, but which are not marked by major crisis; and on the other hand, surges in government debt attributable to wars or financial crises, as in the current situation.

Consolidation by changing policy in non-crisis conditions

In these situations, successful consolidation has most often been initiated following the election of a new government in the aftermath of an electoral campaign fought on the issue. Even if this government is subsequently replaced, the same fiscal efforts are continued. Thus it betokens a political turn involving a long haul, and requiring popular support. This was the case in Denmark (1983), Australia (1984) and Canada (1993). In the two Swedish consolidations initiated in 1981 and 1993, the government that pursued the policy of budgetary stabilization was not the one that had started it, revealing a kind of bipartisan social pact conferring legitimacy on the goal pursued. In the United States, the fiscal consolidation initiated by Bill Clinton in 1993, with a Democratic majority, was pursued with a Republican majority until 2000. In Japan, tight fiscal policy was implemented from 1980 to 1991 in conditions of political continuity, and succeeded in restoring a budget surplus from 1987 to 1991.

In most of these cases (with the exception of Australia), the success of the fiscal effort derived from the fact that it was initiated when growth had been restored following a recession, and not during the recession. Prior closure of the output gap was a condition of success. In France after 1980, by contrast, the turn to competitive disinflation in 1983 put a lasting damper on growth and defeated the fiscal effort, so that the government debt-to-GDP ratio continued to rise.

Consolidation after wars or financial crises

As regards the aftermath of wars, an interesting comparison can be made in the case of the UK in two different historical eras. Following the Napoleonic Wars and the restoration of the gold standard in 1821, on the one hand, and following the Second World War, on the other, levels of government debt were comparable – around 260 per cent of GDP, which is much higher than the current level. In the first era – that is, under the constraint of the gold standard, capital mobility, price stability, and even mild persistent deflation until 1848 – it took forty years to reduce the debt to 100 per cent of GDP. After the Second World War, in a financial system controlled by the state, the same reduction was achieved in twenty years. Prudential regulation and controls on international capital movements made possible maximum reduction of nominal interest rates and attainment of negative real interest rates – the principal factor in reducing government debt – in economic conditions that were compatible with growth despite high levels of debt.

The same situation obtained in France after each of the world wars. In both instances, the debt ratio decreased very rapidly, thanks to inflation and depreciation of the franc between 1920 and 1926, and the massive devaluations in 1948 and 1949 whose anticipation fuelled inflation, bringing massively negative real interest rates in its wake.

In the case of financial crises, the rise in government debt results from the prior excessive accumulation of unsustainable private debt, which undermines bank balance sheets – either directly, in the case of 'normal' finance, or indirectly, through the collapse of the conduits and other special vehicles put in place by the banks to conceal their excessive risk-taking in the casino finance of the 2000s. There is then no chance of consolidating government debt without prior stabilization of the banks' financial situation. This can be achieved through intervention in the immediate wake of the crisis, and fiscal consolidation may then be premature. This was true of Sweden and Finland after the financial crisis of 1991–92, and in Iceland after the 2008 crisis. By contrast, political procrastination under pressure from banking lobbies in Japan after the financial crisis of 1990, and in the eurozone after that of 2008, concealing banks' latent losses and pretending they were healthy, paralyzed any strong recovery in growth and aggravated the burden of government debt.

The Japanese experience is particularly illuminating. From 1991 to 2002, its debt grew inexorably because of a fall in receipts, while expenditure increased only slowly. The collapse in the price of property and stock market assets financed by enterprises with very high bank credit leverage, thanks to the extremely low interest rates of 1986–90, placed the banks in a position of quasi-insolvency.[5] But it took the repercussions of the Asian crisis to induce the public authorities to compel the banks to clean up their balance sheets and restructure to terminate the banking crisis in 2004. Corporate debt reduction, initiated in 1998, continued so that in 2003 growth could be restarted, albeit modestly, and deflation ended. Growth was too weak, however, and the rise in inflation too low to reduce the government debt ratio. It remained on a plateau from 2005 to 2008. The room for manoeuvre to absorb the repercussions of the Western crisis was too limited. That is why the contraction in international trade resulting from the Western financial crisis plunged Japan back into recession and deflation, causing a big rise in the government debt ratio in 2009.

The behaviour of the eurozone governments is similar to that of the Japanese government: denial of banking problems and maintenance of the vicious circle between bank debt and government debt – more generally, an inability to reduce private sector debt. It was only in 2012 (see Chapter 5) that the idea of banking union started to be implemented. But its completion has provoked endless disagreement and procrastination. As long as banking union is not completed, attempts at fiscal consolidation cannot succeed in reversing the burden of government debt in the countries where finance is most damaged.

Fiscal consolidation depends on the economic and financial environment

Historical comparison between epochs when fiscal policy has sought to consolidate government debt in France demonstrates that the economic environment is decisive. In other words, fiscal policy alone is incapable of reversing the rise in the debt-to-GDP ratio. What is required is a buoyant economic environment. This must be created through a coherent combination of all components of economic policy. Decisive for the reduction in government debt between 1890 and 1913 was the fall in real interest rates; between 1920 and 1926, a fall in nominal rates, inflation and currency depreciation played this role; and from 1950 to 1983, controlled nominal rates with sustained inflation did so. In the last period, the other positive determinant was growth, which was systematically above the average interest rate on government debt for more than thirty years.[6]

The abiding decline in the government debt ratio after the Second World War extended beyond France. The Bretton Woods system was conceived to maintain state control of finance, so as to place it at the service of the economy. This made possible much higher growth rates than those posted in the context of liberalized finance after 1980. Capital controls reinforced the attraction of saving for the domestic economy ('home bias'). Banks' compulsory reserves were high for prudential reasons. Not being remunerated, they amounted to an implicit tax on banks. Financial institutions, whether banks or not, were encouraged to hold national government debt. Households were similarly encouraged, because rates on bank deposits were inferior to rates on Treasury bonds. Negative real interest rates were vectors of a progressive liquidation of the debt, creating a transfer from creditors to governments. From 1950 to 1980, real interest rates on government securities in most countries were often negative, and invariably below growth rates.

Sustainability of Government Debt in the Face of Private Debt Reduction

Let us not forget that private debt is what steers economic growth through the financial cycle. In an economy dominated by financial markets, the growth regime is fostered by the cumulative imbalances that constitute the expansionary phase of the financial cycle. It is the reversal in these imbalances after the fork of the financial crisis that propels government debt into potential unsustainability.

Periods of recession or stagnation are not systematically periods of debt reduction in the economy. Private actors want to reduce their debt or are compelled to, but the drop in income counteracts debt reduction, because debtors cannot allocate sufficient income to interest payments on outstanding debts, or to absorbing losses stemming from the fall in the value of their assets. In the eurozone, households in countries greatly affected by the real estate debacle have reduced debt by abandoning their properties, which banks have repossessed at prices far below their original value. In Spain, where the housing sector ballooned absurdly, its implosion swept away a large number of property developers and construction companies. Enterprises have reduced debt by going under – hence by destroying capital. In other countries, particularly France, banks supported enterprises in major difficulties, renewing their loans so as not to have to acknowledge losses. But corporate investment declined, so that increased household saving could not be absorbed in the domestic private sector. Germany did it by inflating its trade surplus, which was tantamount to exporting excess savings. In countries with a current account deficit, such as France, the public sector had to increase its deficit to avoid an economic depression. States played the role of borrowers of last resort, and thereby significantly increased their debt.

Government debt thus has a stabilizing, counter-cyclical influence. In this way, it assists monetary policy. The latter must therefore ultimately help the development of government debt to remain on a sustainable path by keeping interest rates very low long after the private sector has begun to recover. A precise definition of a sustainable trajectory is now required.

It has already been said that the condition of sustainability is not the convergence of the debt-to-GDP ratio on an optimal equilibrium level that does not exist. The path is sustainable if the debt's discounted value tends towards zero when its horizon tends towards infinity (see Inset 6.1, p. 154)

The discounted value of the gross sustainable debt at long-term equilibrium is the sum of the discounted future primary surpluses that finance it. Anticipated future primary balances (or budget balances minus net interest payments) are therefore the relevant factor in studying sustainability. The discount rate also plays a crucial role. The lower the discount factor, which varies inversely with the discount rate – that is, the higher the discount rate, equal to the difference between the real interest paid on government debt and the economy's growth rate – the less surpluses in the distant future count in the value of sustainable debt (see Inset 6.1). When holders of government debt fear that the debt is unsustainable (as in the cases of Greece, Portugal and Ireland in 2010, and of Spain and Italy in 2011 and 2012), they seek to sell bonds on this debt. They cause the interest rate to rise, since potential purchasers demand high-risk premiums. The rise in interest rates on government securities, which are the pivots of financial markets, impacts on all lending to the private sector. The upshot is a damper on growth, even a recession, and hence lower fiscal receipts. The government budget deficit grows rather than declining, swelling public debt and further increasing the anxiety of states' private creditors. A vicious circle may then set in, liable to lead the public finances onto an unsustainable path. To maintain sustainability, the central bank has to intervene. It can do so either directly, by buying government bonds (as did the ECB in 2010 in the case of Greece, Portugal and Ireland), or indirectly, by lending banks unlimited liquidity at quasi-zero interest rates so that banks are encouraged to buy government securities. But it is also necessary for states in crisis to act rapidly. In these acute crisis situations, sustainability involves short-term consolidation of the public finances which lost growth – exacerbated by private-sector debt reduction – makes difficult. Central bank aid is indispensable, but it may not be enough. In the case of Greece, the creditor states and the Central Bank should have negotiated a plan to restructure the debt that would have significantly reduced its cost: cancellation of a sufficient sum to return the country to a sustainable path, rescheduling by converting existing debt into very-long-term bonds so as to spread payments with a cut in interest rates.

Thus, not all government debt paths are sustainable. The domain of sustainable paths is separated from that of divergent paths by a borderline path, called a 'saddle-point path'. The size of an indebted country's domain of sustainability crucially depends on the discount rate. In contrast to unsustainable paths, there are paths where sustainability does not require stringent fiscal effort because the government has prevailed in its pursuit of sufficiently high growth. If the growth rate is higher than the real interest rate, fiscal receipts, which are roughly proportional to GDP in conditions of constant fiscal policy, increase more quickly than the interest paid on the stock of debt. This prompts a mechanical reduction in the debt, unless the primary deficit grows unduly – that is, unless the state is genuinely a big spender. If this were the case, however, interest rates would go back up. Between these two options, we find intermediate situations where the real interest rate is higher than the growth rate, but where the difference is small.

The state has to pursue a policy of debt consolidation. But it can spread it over time, so that fiscal efforts to reduce the deficit are proportionate and do not kill off growth.

Inset 6.1: Government Debt Accounting

Accounting for fiscal expenditure and receipts in the annual budget is analysed as follows:

$H-T+iF = \Delta D+\Delta M$

H is total public expenditure, T total fiscal receipts, D the stock of sovereign bonds, ΔD the net annual cash flow, and ΔM the monetization of the public deficit by the central bank. The left-hand side is therefore the deficit, while the right-hand side is the financing.

This accounting equation can be expressed as a percentage of nominal GDP:

$h-\tau+(i-\pi-g)d-1=\Delta d+\Delta m+(\pi+g)m-1$

The primary deficit as a percentage of GDP does not depend on the capital market:

$b=h-\tau-\Delta m-(\pi+g)m-1$

where $((\pi+g)m-1)$. is the seigniorage

We may define the real interest rate ex post adjusted for growth:

$\rho=i-\pi-g$

The dynamic of the debt is described by the discrete-time differential equation:

$b+\rho d-1=\Delta d$

This equation is solved by iteration for a debt during n periods:

$$d_t = E_t\delta_{t,n}d_{t+n} - E_t\sum_{j=1}^{j=n}\delta_{t,j}b_{t+j}$$

The discount factor in n periods in the future is:

$$\delta_{t,n} = \prod_{s=1}^{s=n} (1 + \rho_{t+s})^{-1}$$

We may observe that *the discount rate of the government debt is equal to the difference between the average real interest rate paid on the debt in circulation (function of the structure of the debt) and the economy's growth rate.* The discounted value of the debt in t is therefore equal to the discounted anticipated value of the debt in t+n increased by the discount value of the primary deficits (when b>0) between t and t+n or reduced by the discount value of the primary surpluses (when b<0).

The condition of sustainability is obtained when n→∞ Government debt is sustainable if its discount value ? 0 when the horizon of the debt tends towards infinity. The condition is as follows:

$$\lim n \to \infty E_t \delta_{t+n} d_{t+n} = 0$$

This is the condition of transversality, which signifies that the debt/GDP ratio must follow a path tending towards a stationary state for the public finances to be sustainable. It is not necessary for it to converge on a predetermined maximum (60 per cent or some other figure). Its value depends on the pattern of future primary surpluses:

$$d^* = -\lim_{n\to\infty} E_t \sum_{j=1}^{j=n} \delta_{t,j} b_{t+.}$$

In the wake of a financial crisis, a significant amount of debt has been transferred from the private to the public sector. Too onerous and rapid a fiscal effort, as in Europe from 2011 to 2013, reduces the economy's trend growth rate for a considerable period of time. This raises the discount rate, thus reducing the discount factor, which varies inversely with it. As a result, the discounted weight of remote future surpluses becomes negligible. The domain of sustainable debt paths shrinks. The track of future debt can then become unsustainable, and a default may occur. But it is not the debt level per se that produces this result, contrary to what Carmen Reinhart and Kenneth Rogoff claim. It is subsequent macroeconomic policy, if it is not appropriate to this level of debt.

The importance of the discount rate demonstrates what the historical episodes have afforded us a glimpse of. To consolidate government debt successfully in a good environment – that is, bringing down unemployment – what is required is a policy for growth over a sufficiently extended timescale. This is the opposite of the course followed by eurozone countries in recent years. The longer the adjustment period, hence the lower the discount rate, the more room for manoeuvre the government has to implement a credible programme.

The results to date lead to the following recommendation. To be understood by the markets and to keep the public finances on a sustainable path, it is necessary to commit to a medium-term programme that can be revised in the light of significant changes in growth and interest rates, and justified in the context of the scenarios identified above. Furthermore, macroeconomic policies must be designed so as to enlarge the spectrum of sustainable paths by optimal steering of growth and interest rates. This obviously involves dialogue between the central bank and the state. In the eurozone, this means the ECB and states associated and coordinated by a body whose contours will be defined in Chapter 7. Before that, I shall illustrate some plausible consolidation scenarios for the French economy, taking 2015 as a horizon. We know that the two key variables are the ten-year real interest rate and the growth rate.

Government Debt Paths Depending on Growth and Interest Scenarios for France

The work done by Thomas Brand can be found in the report on government debt for the CDC.[7] Here I will present the results that are directly connected to the preceding theoretical analysis.

The simulations employ a dynamic macroeconomic model of the French economy, in which exogenous economic magnitudes and parameters are calibrated on the basis of national accounting data. The model is of an open economy where production depends on three factors: labour, physical corporate capital, and energy. Total factor productivity depends on public capital. Private consumption is determined by a propensity to consume out of disposable household income.

Social expenditures (pensions, health, family) depend on demography, and an exogenous rate per recipient deriving from social policy. The same applies to unemployment benefit per unemployed person. The number of unemployed is determined by macroeconomic equilibrium. Other expenditures, as well as fiscal receipts, are proportional to GDP. The cost of government debt depends on its maturity, which is around seven years. Every year, one-seventh of the debt inherited from the past is paid off at the market base interest rate (ten-year rate), and the remaining six-sevenths are paid at the past effective rate. It is assumed that the Central Bank has a ten-year target rate that it controls. For a given rate of growth of GDP, the model calculates the difference each year between receipts and expenditure, including interest, which determines increase or reduction in the debt.

In line with the theoretical analysis, the scenarios for government debt consolidation are envisaged on the basis of growth rates and interest rates. Three growth hypotheses are entertained in principle: a pessimistic scenario with a trend growth rate of 1 per cent per annum over ten years; a middling scenario with a growth rate of 1.5 per cent; and an optimistic scenario with a growth rate of 2 per cent.

These estimates coincide with the available forecasts, which generally situate potential growth between 1 and 2 per cent. The OECD and IMF forecast average growth of 1.5 per cent in France up to 2020, and the European Commission forecasts growth of the order of 1.4 per cent. In its assessment of April 2013, the Haut Conseil des Finances Publiques reckoned that estimated potential growth of 1.5 per cent, which underlies public finance forecasts, 'without being unduly optimistic, is hedged round by a number of depressive risks' (longer-lasting effects of the crisis, less positive impact of reforms on growth than the government expects, the impact of fiscal consolidation measures). We may note that average growth between 1990 and 2007 was 1.9 per cent, and growth from 1990 to 2012 was 1.5 per cent.

The optimistic scenario entails the total absorption of the financial crisis, aside from the definitive losses resulting in a GDP level every year lower than it would have been had the financial crisis not occurred. In this scenario, pre-crisis potential growth is restored, and thus the economy is rescued from secular stagnation. The rate of structural unemployment could fall back to 7 per cent. Such a scenario involves very profound changes in the economy that will be discussed in Chapters 8 and 9. In the current state of the French political landscape and the paralyzing governance of Europe, it may be regarded as highly unlikely.

The pessimistic scenario parks the economy in secular stagnation. In these circumstances, the unemployment rate remains blocked at 9.5 per cent of the working population.

Finally, the middling scenario is the most interesting. The unemployment rate can fall to 8 per cent on condition that the rate of investment and the rate of utilization of productive capacity return to levels close to their average for the years 1990–2007. It is ambitious, but not completely out of reach.

What are the consequences for the level and pattern of government debt in 2025? To calculate it, we must cross-reference growth scenarios with projections for the ten-year interest rate. The effective, hence nominal, interest rate on French government debt has tended to fall, since preparations for joining the eurozone, from 6 per cent to 3 per cent in mid 2014 (the ten-year market rate being around 2.5 per cent).

The middling scenario for ten-year interest rates on government debt projects maintenance of the interest rate at 2.8 per cent. With projected inflation at 1.5 per cent, this boils down to envisaging a real interest rate of 1.3 per cent – that is, close to the growth rate. On the other hand, this hypothesis is not compatible with the pessimistic scenario. In a context of secular stagnation, the ECB would keep its own interest rate in the region of 0 per cent, which would lead to the ten-year rate continuing to decline to 1.8 per cent. Inflation would stabilize around 0.5 per cent for a real rate equivalent to that of the middling scenario, but for lower growth, since low inflation forms part of secular stagnation. The optimistic scenario, meanwhile, would see a rise in rates to 3.8 per cent.

We therefore have a pessimistic scenario with growth of 1 per cent and an effective nominal ten-year interest rate of 1.8 and a middling scenario with a growth rate of 1.5 per cent and a ten-year interest rate of 2.8 per cent. Three fiscal strategies might be envisaged. The first, the status quo – that is, no additional attempt at fiscal contraction over and above what has already been implemented – is not realistic. But its outcome furnishes a marker that enables us to measure what is achieved in government debt reduction by pursuing consolidation policies. A strategy of rapid consolidation is defined by a structural fiscal effort of 0.75 per cent of GDP every year until 2020 – that is, an attempt is made to reduce the structural budget deficit (excluding the fiscal impact of the conjuncture) by this amount every year, or 4.5 per cent of total GDP between now and 2020. A different strategy is a gradual fiscal consolidation of 0.4 per cent of GDP every year until 2025, or the same total fiscal effort, but spread over ten years rather than being concentrated into five.

The results of the simulation are assembled in Table 6.1 on p. 162. They concern not only the level of the government debt-to-GDP ratio in 2025, but also some indication as to the development of this ratio after 2025. The latter is assessed in terms of the difference between the primary fiscal balance (excluding interest payments) denoted by PB and the primary balance stabilizing the debt in 2025 (SPB). Because the difference (PB – SPB) is positive, the primary surplus is higher than the stabilizing balance. This indicates that government debt as a percentage of GDP continues to decline after 2025. The scale of the difference indicates the speed of the debt reduction.

Which course is preferable? It is clear that fiscal consolidation is required. The status quo results in perpetual increases in government debt, and thus places it on a divergent path. It would only be compatible with a strong growth scenario, and would yield the same results as the historical consolidations of the 1950s and '60s. If growth is strong and above the real interest rate, government debt is automatically absorbed. Given the straitjacket of the rules binding the eurozone economies, however, nothing in current policy warrants our envisaging a return to strong growth. It therefore comes down to a choice about the pace of fiscal consolidation, in the knowledge that, the more rapid the consolidation, the more the pessimistic scenario is likely to impose itself at the expense of the middling scenario.

We are therefore led instead to compare the pessimistic scenario and rapid consolidation, on the one hand, with the middling scenario and gradual consolidation, on the other. The two scenarios are not equivalent. The middling scenario, with its stronger growth, has the potential for a larger decrease in government debt after 2025 with a gradual consolidation than the pessimistic scenario with a rapid consolidation. Furthermore, the reduction of government debt is not, or should not be, the ultimate objective of economic policy. Bringing down unemployment is a much more important social objective, but little weight is attached to it by governments in France, in particular. In order to tackle it, after all, it is necessary to undertake public investment, whose growth effects make themselves felt in the long run. In addition, a return to prioritizing investment involves restructuring the budget in favour of discretionary expenditure, in contrast to wages, which are statutory expenditure,

or social benefits, which are expenditure prescribed by legislation or negotiated between social partners. Restructuring
the budget in favour of investment is therefore difficult. It
succeeded in Sweden in the 1990s because of a vast political
consensus on the principle, parliamentary control at every
stage of the reform, and commitment by social partners to
its implementation in enterprises. Unfortunately, none of
these conditions obtains in France.

Table 6.1: Government Debt, Primary Balance (PB)
and Stabilizing Primary Balance in 2025 (SPB)

en % du PIB

	Status quo	Rapid Consolidation	Slow consolidation
Low scenario	111	73	84
		SP=2,1 SPS=0,9	SP=2,1 SPS=1,1
Central scenario	102	64	75
		SP=3,6 SPS=0,9	SP=3,6 SPS=1,1

Source: calculations by Thomas Brand, in
Dettes publiques en zone euro, p. 106.

This simulation has been carried out for France, but it
concerns the whole eurozone. The lesson is that a community of choice in favour of growth is indispensable. In
Chapters 8 and 9, I shall endeavour to define the form it
might take. But any growth policy is conditional on the
institutional process of completing the euro. In Chapter 5
we explored possible developments in the financial sphere.
We must now see what is possible in the fiscal sphere.

7.

How Can Fiscal Union Be Advanced?

We saw in Chapter 2 that there have been some not insignificant institutional initiatives since 2010. However, the Fiscal Union Treaty as currently conceived does not allow for consideration of the inter-temporal aspect of government debt, which determines sustainable paths. In Chapter 6, I defined what a sustainable debt is for a state. How can this be extended to a set of states bound together by a currency? It might be said that it is enough to do what Hamilton did in the United States in 1790.

In the 1780s, the public finances of the confederated states that had won the War of Independence were in a parlous condition, and there was great disparity between them. The failure to pool war debts made monetary and hence political division likely. There were violent disagreements in Congress. Pitting two camps against one another, the debate, familiar since Antiquity, concerned the organization of public powers: political federalism or a confederation of states. Supporters of the latter were violently opposed to transferring debt to the federal government. They were not without arguments. Should such a transfer occur, it would reward speculators who had bought debt from investors in difficulty. Some states would be relieved of a greater burden than others. Central executive power would be strengthened at the expense of Congress and the states. The most vehement orator in defence of this line was James Madison, who was spokesman for the southern states. He feared that centralizing the debt would put states under the heel of a remote, irresponsible government. In addition, he claimed that pooling would force virtuous states to come to the aid of impecunious states, and that this represented a threat to the young republic.

It is not difficult to hear the echo of current German rhetoric in these arguments. How many times have we heard contemptuous statements about impecunious, irresponsible countries reported by the German press? And we witness rejection of any fiscal solidarity and a refusal to pool debt and issue euro bonds, which are repudiated with horror. Relying on the Basic Law behind the shield of the Constitutional Court in Karlsruhe, the same political arguments as Madison's are marshalled: the threat of a perversion of democracy by a distant, irresponsible power.

By contrast, Alexander Hamilton commended the efficacy of a unified securities market. In 1790, he was appointed treasury secretary. He proposed to centralize states' debts by issuing new bonds backed by credible fiscal receipts. He maintained that creating a national debt would attract investors and form a very strong social bond for the union.[1] Hamilton prevailed. The debt was centralized and financed by federal taxation.

Obviously, this historical reference merely serves to indicate that there is nothing new about current arguments. They actually date back much further than the episode of the unification of the United States. Anti-federalists adopted the ideas of Montesquieu, which were themselves inspired by Plato. In a confederation of states, governments are closer to the people. But the eurozone has already taken a major step towards federalism by establishing a single currency. We then re-encounter Hamilton's argument: Can monetary unity proceed without unified government debt? This is also the argument developed in Chapter 2: the social contract represented by money is complete only if the latter is the counterpart of the social debt whose authorized signatory is the state.

If one believes that this organic link is the political horizon of the European project, the progressive approach employed in Chapter 5 to examine how effective common institutions can be created in the financial sphere also applies to the fiscal sphere. It must be based on what has already been accomplished with the 2012 Fiscal Treaty to advance along the road of integration, assuming that the various parties' arguments are not antagonistic; otherwise the desire to preserve the euro would be a dead letter.

The golden thread consists in identifying a course that transforms European governance in a way that is acceptable to member-states while enriching the democratic content of the institutional advances to be accomplished. At the fiscal level proper, this means making the transition from rules-based coordination to collective action.

The theory of public finances has shown that the state's economic functions are of three kinds: stabilization, redistribution and allocation.[2] The function of stabilization takes the form of a mechanism ensuring against asymmetric shocks. As the last section of Chapter 3 outlined, controlling them involves countries whose policies impact on the macroeconomic equilibria of other countries taking their interests into account. The function of allocation implies restructuring the European budget in favour of the 'competitiveness and growth' objective, and authorizing the Union to go into debt by issuing bonds via the European Fund, defined in Chapter 5. Redistribution is the set of transfer mechanisms aimed at reducing income inequalities between social groups or regions.

Collective action is feasible in each of these areas. Direct fiscal redistribution in Europe is currently an inviolable taboo for Germany. But the functions are not independent. Progress in the other two has indirect redistributive effects that may be positive. I shall concern myself first with the problems of stabilization. Next I shall return to the issue of allocation. It concerns public investment and, more generally, financing the structural investment I have already discussed in Chapter 5. Finally, I shall return to the political problem. What form should the democratic foundation of this institutional system take?

From Coordination by Rules to Collective Action: The Thorny Problem of Stabilization

A major problem in a monetary union between very different countries is what economists call 'asymmetric shocks'. Country A, which suffers, for example, a recessionary shock because it wants to reduce its budget deficit unilaterally, causes its partners to suffer repercussions in the form of a reduction in its imports, and hence in their exports to country A. In a monetary union, the affected countries cannot avail themselves of devaluation of the exchange rate to offset the shock, making their exports less expensive. If they want to compensate for the shock, they must pursue an expansionary fiscal policy that might not suit them and that, in any event, will create a deficit in the balance of payments if it was hitherto in balance. For its part, monetary policy is impotent because it is determined on the basis of the union's average macroeconomic circumstances. It is therefore too tight for countries with low inflation and spare capacity, and too loose for countries with high inflation that are overheating, in the presence of asymmetric shocks. It results in real interest rates that are too high in the first type of country and too low in the second, incentivizing private capital to aggravate the imbalances.

We can see that economic interdependence creates what is called an externality – a repercussion which markets do not absorb effectively. Our experience has demonstrated that it was worse than that: the financial markets aggravated imbalances rather than absorbing them. Chapter 3 addressed this process. Since the creation of the euro, divergences between economies have been amplified by massive capital movements from the countries of the North to countries of the South, in accordance with the picture in Figure 3.1b (p. 66). Government debt was irrelevant in this process, since the accumulated imbalances derived in their entirety from private debt. A symmetrical phenomenon emerged with the Greek crisis. The flight of capital affected a group of solvent countries when it accumulated in Germany and a number of north European satellite countries. The result was an enormous divergence in interest rates, causing deep recession in the countries of southern Europe. Germany's refusal to pursue an offsetting expansionary policy condemned countries with fragile debts to the unilateral implementation of cruelly deflationary policies. The result was a general drop in inflation, and the sequences described in Chapter 1 (Figure 1.4), leading to very low growth.

The political authorities and the European Commission systematically underestimated these externalities, which boiled down to denying the incompletion of the euro. To this end, they advanced an economic theory of 'optimum currency areas'.[3] The creation of the European Single Market, crowned by the single currency, was intended to prompt structural changes making the eurozone an optimum currency area, where automatic mechanisms offset asymmetric shocks. The question is therefore as follows: What mechanisms can compensate for the loss of the exchange rate as an adjustment variable to stabilize economies facing asymmetric shocks?

Theoreticians have suggested various desiderata, which are not relevant to the eurozone. The first is geographical migration of labour. Migration from country A, with underemployment, to country B, suffering inflationary pressures, absorbs unemployment in A and reduces inflationary pressures in B. This is a purely theoretical idea at a European level. Many reasons prevent workers and their families from following conjunctural fluctuations in the labour market between countries. Another possible adjustment, favoured by European doxa, is an 'internal devaluation'. It involves a decline in wages in country A, suffering from underemployment, sufficient to increase competitiveness and stimulate exports. But the exchange rate is, by definition, a symmetrical adjustment. A devaluation in A is a revaluation in B, and hence a damper on the rise in prices. To obtain the same result, the fall in wages in A must not be absorbed by exporters' profit margins. In addition, wages must be as flexible as exchange rates. Once again, this is not possible for a multitude of social and institutional reasons. Experience in Greece, Portugal and Spain since 2010 shows that 'internal devaluation' is possible – but only at the cost of massive unemployment (25 per cent of the working population in Spain) and enormous impoverishment. This has nothing to do with a stabilizing adjustment.

We therefore return to our starting-point. For effective adjustment to occur in the face of asymmetric shocks in a monetary union, economic policy must be coordinated by countries. Automatic rules are no substitute – they are neither flexible nor binding, and are therefore not adapted to the variability of economic circumstances. Furthermore, they only function in a restrictive direction. No automatic rule will compel the German government to pursue a policy of wage increases or greater public expenditure to offset wage deflation in another group of countries. In principle, there is a limit to countries' current account surpluses in the dispositions guiding European macroeconomic monitoring. However, since a German surplus of 7.5 per cent of GDP in 2013 did not prompt official registration – and still less a request for correction – the adjustment disposition relative to this limit is, to all intents and purposes, null and void.

We must therefore argue differently in order to advance the Fiscal Stability Treaty (SCGT). Governments must be able to have confidence in one another, thanks to an assessment of macroeconomic and fiscal situations that takes account of these forms of interdependence, and is conducted by independent bodies of experts. On this basis, a fiscal agency with representatives from national parliaments – hence different from the Commission – must define the approach of a coordinated policy, to be validated by the European Council and implemented by governments. The 'European Semester', which is precisely intended for coordination, suits the development of such procedures.

As it stands, the European Semester is a modest affair. Elaboration of member-states' annual finance laws is preceded by toing-and-froing between national treasuries and the Commission to compare drafts, and to ensure that they are fully compatible with the medium-term stability programmes to which governments are signed up. But democracy finds no toehold here, because national parliaments have no coordinating body.

Finally, the stabilization policies selected must be compatible with the principles of government debt consolidation highlighted in Chapter 6.

High Councils of Public Finances and their networking

The establishment of high councils of public finances in countries that have ratified the Fiscal Union Treaty is an innovation whose import and potential we need to understand. Well before the 2012 Treaty, independent budgetary institutions existed in a number of countries – for example, the Congressional Budget Office in the United States, the Central Planning Bureau in the Netherlands, or the Haut Conseil de Finance in Belgium. All these bodies, old or new, are evaluative bodies that issue opinions and recommendations. They combine expertise and independence: none is a decision-maker. They make fiscal projections themselves if they possess a full technical staff, or assess the plausibility of government forecasts in the light of existing forecasts if they do not. Their aim is to indicate the future impact of current budget decisions on the sustainability of government debt. The guarantee of independence they bring with them does not stem exclusively from their legal status. The latter provides for appointment procedures based on the professionalism of the persons sought. Mandates are not renewable. Ministers and civil servants answer the Council's questions, but do not interfere in its work. Finally, the incentive for their members is to build and maintain a reputation, not to be influenced by some political consideration.

Since governments have committed themselves to respecting fiscal rules – as with the Fiscal Stability Treaty – an independent body in each country makes public its verdict on its fiscal policy's conformity to these rules. First, it informs parliament about the macroeconomic environment of the annual budget, because it analyses the prospects and explicitly examines a wide range of forecasts from different institutes, public and private, national and foreign. Second, it provides information to private economic actors, international institutions and foreign public decision-makers. Its public views offer information and independent analysis to a wide range of actors. It can be argued that high councils of public finances are the best ratings agencies for states, since they are obviously better informed and carry out much more profound analyses than the three American ratings agencies.

The Councils' role could be developed if governments advanced the Fiscal Stability Treaty beyond the simplistic and dangerous rules currently in force. In fact, these rules take no account either of the contingencies inherent in uncertainty, or the specificities of the financing of public investment. Independent councils can assess conformity with more complex, contingent rules. They can offer an authoritative view on governments' need to determine whether it is wise to deviate from a simplistic rule in given conditions. This is currently the case when the structural deficit to which a government is committed assumes potential growth that is dubious. This would form part of a clear definition of the role of rules. Fiscal policy cannot take the form of automatic piloting. It resembles the model of the restricted discretionary policy of central banks. Isomorphic operational logics would make it possible to guide the relations that should exist between monetary policy and fiscal policy.

Creating a network of councils in a European Budget Agency or Institute, or whatever one wishes to call it, would be a further step in fiscal coordination, to improve the quality of the eurozone's fiscal policy and facilitate the Eurogroup's dialogue with the ECB in defining a policy mix that has hitherto been lacking. National parliaments could participate directly in fiscal coordination if the opinion issued by the Institute was examined and discussed in a conference of representatives from the national parliaments' finance committees. A modicum of democracy would thus be reintroduced into a two-way procedure currently utterly lacking in any.

A cyclical stabilization mechanism in the eurozone

This book has frequently noted how harmful blind observance of rigid fiscal rules is. The absence of macroeconomic stabilization in countries renders any return to long-term growth sufficient to bring about a sustained improvement in employment most unlikely. The European stabilization mechanism aims to have a long-term impact on employment, as well as moderating cyclical fluctuations in the eurozone.

Several mechanisms can be envisaged. One possibility is a form of European unemployment insurance.[4] It presupposes a European labour contract negotiated between governments, with which it would be combined. The contract would be permanent, and would authorize flexibility in lay-offs with a no-claims bonus clause for enterprises, as in any insurance contract. The labour contract must be integrated into national laws to enable workers to choose the type of contract they prefer. Choosing this contract would provide access rights to European unemployment insurance, in addition to benefits from national unemployment insurance. A European fund would be needed to regulate transfers. It should seek to balance its accounts over the economic cycle of the eurozone as a whole, varying contribution rates, so that it is a pure stabilization mechanism without sustained income redistribution between countries.

However, if we make so bold as to believe that a dose of solidarity between countries trying to work their way towards full fiscal union would be welcome, and if, in any event, we wish to avoid a perverse anti-redistribution, it would be appropriate to modulate the compensation formula. For countries with the highest levels of compensation to contribute more than the average, and those with the lowest less, it would suffice to calculate the pay-out on the basis of the average national wage.

This European unemployment insurance mechanism is nevertheless demanding in terms of European integration, in that it requires a European work contract. Over and above the transfer mechanism proper, reform aims to initiate harmonization of the labour market. In addition, it operates on the unemployment level. To the extent that cycles are correlated, the underlying fiscal rule does not prevent aggregate unemployment in the eurozone being above the 'natural' unemployment rate that is supposed to represent full employment. It follows that it must be possible for the European insurance fund to be in deficit in a period of aggregate underemployment. It must therefore be possible for it to be covered by a revised European budget, or to issue bonds on the financial market.

To avoid any objection from states to the premature pooling of sovereignty, and hence to propose a pure stabilization mechanism, the Delors-founded association 'Nôtre Europe' has sought to delineate a purely cyclical stabilization mechanism – that is, a mechanism for which the European insurance fund is structurally in balance.[5] The scheme refers to potential GDP to calculate each country's output gap. Transfers are calculated on the basis of relative output gaps.

If output gaps are measured accurately, all countries have a net-zero position over the whole cycle. It follows that transfers are in fact temporary. There is no systematic redistribution in the scheme. In addition, since transfers are calculated on the basis of relative positions within the eurozone, by its very nature the insurance fund is in balance each year. There is no need for European taxes or borrowing to finance it.

However, calculation of output gaps is unreliable. The Commission's estimates do not coincide with those of national governments. This can occasion moral hazard, created by governments seeking to increase their negative relative output gap in order to obtain more transfers, and by governments seeking to minimize their positive relative output gap so as to pay less. Central regulation of the mechanism by the European fiscal agency referred to above is therefore required, adopting output gaps calculated by it and effective control over transfer flows, since the way that funds are spent in countries in deficit influences the size of the multiplier. To achieve control in non-arbitrary fashion, the insurance scheme's purpose must be borne in mind. To stabilize is above all to reduce the social costs of unemployment. It would therefore be best for these funds to place conditions on how they are spent. They should be pre-allocated to national social security systems. The philosophy of the mechanism of relative stabilization on the basis of output gaps thereby approximates to the direct mechanism of unemployment insurance, while resolving the problem of financing.

The Budget and Financing of European Growth

There is a close link between fiscal consolidation and public investment, because the former is a long-term process and the latter improves potential growth. The fall in the rate of public investment in Europe over more than thirty years, noted in Chapter 1 (Figure 1.2), is the best illustration of the abdication of European governments in the face of financial globalization. A reversal in this trend is the starting-point for a common will to construct a new growth regime. It naturally involves rethinking the purposes of the European budget, expanding it and reforming its structure.

Equipping Europe with a European budget worthy of the name

Europe's budget is not large enough, and its resources should be increased to promote competitiveness and innovation. In addition, since Europe is not sovereign, it raises no taxes. The European Parliament does not possess the traditional fiscal power of national parliaments. The budget is therefore supplied exclusively by contributions from member-states.

The European budget represents around 1 per cent of the Union's GDP. With the adoption of the financial framework for the period 2013–20, the European Council managed to reduce it! In truth, the fall has been ongoing. It has declined from 1.2 per cent of GDP in 1993 to 0.95 per cent projected for 2020. Even the Commission's minimum proposal to stabilize it as a share of GDP was rejected. Let us recall that a tax on financial transactions could bring in something of the order of €200 billion per annum, and double the budget's size to 2 per cent of GDP. The main source is the flat-rate contribution of 0.73 per cent of each state's gross national income, which accounts for 65 per cent of total receipts. The other two significant sources are the levy on VAT (transfer of 0.3 per cent of the VAT collected by member-states) and the customs duties collected at the Union's external borders from third-party countries.

Expenditure to improve competitiveness and innovation for growth and jobs accounts for 9 per cent of the budget, or less than 1 per cent of European GDP. This is the expenditure that has been reduced most as a result of austerity in national budgets . . . because it does not yield fiscal returns! It is clear that the European budget is insufficient to help meet the objectives of the Europe 2020 strategy, just as it was for the 2010 strategy formulated at Lisbon in 2000.

As long as the financing of the European budget is not revised, so that it is not dependent exclusively on national contributions, the Commission proposes to resort to borrowing: to finance transport infrastructure through 'project bonds' and to develop public–private partnerships to finance innovation. This is not enough to forge an inclusive European growth model. A model of European solidarity committed to growth has to be invented. For that, obviously, European political projects would have to be developed for the European elections, to enable citizens to see that a common interest and common projects can create jobs – in other words, the opposite of what happened in the 2014 election, which gave free rein to nationalist demagogy. The crisis led to the European budget being complemented by the European Stability Mechanism. But that does not solve the fundamental problem. How can a solidaristic growth policy be forged without an adequate European budget?

Even if one accepts the idea that different mechanisms for financing investment are needed (see Chapter 5), the European budget must be reorientated to serve the stated objectives. The least one can expect of the ambition of advancing economic union is that the European budget should have the size and structure required to finance the

European public goods indispensable to a common plan for growth.

Network industries are European public goods that are the bases of innovation. The development of network industries is essential to galvanizing regions, creating inter-regional interfaces, and generating downstream industry thanks to clustering effects. Yet no structural funds are allocated to innovation! Furthermore, innovation throughout Europe is directly bound up with creating a European labour market through workforce mobility, mutual recognition of qualifications by member-states, and thus training programmes and curricula with European certification. This involves generating technological universities via inter-state cooperation, prioritizing human investment in countries in difficulty, and marketing processes that allow SMEs to innovate throughout Europe. In the energy sector, which is currently in a state of utter confusion because of the contradictory options of the principal member-states, a European energy community must be built with the objectives of a drastic fall in CO_2 emissions and security of supply for all EU countries, and hence solidarity between them. There is therefore an urgent need to negotiate an energy solidarity pact for symbiosis between choices of primary energy sources and the development of intelligent electricity-distribution networks at a European level.

Thus, the renewal of growth in Europe leads to a rethinking of the financing of future investment with a European basis – that is, constructing European financial intermediation that takes the form of supporting Europe's own budgetary resources and financial intermediation in which public finance and public guarantees from Europe as a whole draw in private financial actors. Europe must be in a position both to have its own fiscal resources and to take on debt in international markets in the form of eurobonds.

Issuing eurobonds to finance European growth

Should the eurozone countries genuinely decide to make restoring growth a long-term objective, they must combine to produce public goods and boost private investment. It follows that Europe must be able to create eurobonds in the framework of a European fiscal policy for growth. These bonds must not be confused with those proposed to pool member-states' government debt. They would be issued by the European Investment Fund, whose role was set out in Chapter 5, under the control of the European Parliament and with the European budget as security.

Intended for institutional investors to finance investment projects of European significance, these Eurobonds have nothing to do with the pooling of government debts by substituting a union-level debt for national debts – a proposal that is controversial. They involve financing new capital, not converting old debts. In this way, a direct connection would be established between the European budget and financial intermediation intended to finance long-term growth.

The Horizon of Political Union: What Democratic Legitimacy?

The progressive institutional changes described from Chapter 5 onwards are meaningful solely in the context of a completion of the euro. A complete currency entails an organic link with a political sovereignty. In Europe, this sovereignty can only be democratic in Tocqueville's sense of participatory government – that is, concretely involving citizens. This was Jean Monnet's ambition: bringing citizens together to avert wrenching rivalry between states. The modest course followed since the start of the European project has been called the community approach (*démarche communautaire*).

Since the Maastricht Treaty, and even more so since the euro's advent, the *démarche communautaire* has been stifled and the distance between European rituals and citizens has become such that the convulsions of the eurozone crisis are incomprehensible to the uninitiated. If democracy can be defined as government by debate, it has forsaken existing political procedures at a European level. In fact, European governance has been usurped by intergovernmental clashes followed by painful compromises, and by the bureaucrats of the Commission, who lack democratic legitimacy.

Faced with the fundamental choices required to put Europe on the road to inclusive, sustainable growth, only a broad conception of democracy can succeed: political participation, dialogue, public interaction. European governance will not be improved merely by organizing periodic European elections for a parliament bereft of sovereignty.

In a recent work, the German philosopher Jürgen Habermas put the eurozone crisis in perspective, employing concepts from political science.[6] The radical deficiencies of monetary union derive from the lack of capacity for political regulation at a European level. The method of intergovernmental coordination in small steps is both ineffective and undemocratic, hence illegitimate. Government decisions cannot be legitimate in the absence of democratic validation. The tension between the economic and financial imperatives of action to solve the crisis, and the absence of a European political power democratically controlled by a European constitutional law, are leading to Europe's political fragmentation. For intergovernmental coordination cannot withstand the centrifugal forces accentuated by the crisis.

That is why the Europe Union finds itself at a fork in the road. There is a democratic deficit because the democracy rooted in nation-states is submerged by globalized private financial interests. Because they increasingly determine national policies, and hence strongly influence citizens' lives, the compromises negotiated by governments, which (except in Germany) are imposed without public debate, degrade democracy in the member-states. Readers may remember autumn 2011, when a referendum called in Greece – and the least that could be done given the gravity of the situation was to consult the people – was cancelled, under joint pressure from Berlin and Brussels. They feared the further contagion that rampant financial speculation would cause. The preponderance of financial fundamentalism over democracy has never been so patent.

Democracy is a self-referential, non-transcendent process: citizens regard it as legitimate to obey laws of which they are the authors. This can only work if the political process is inclusive. Yet the procedure is majority rule. It must therefore be accompanied by a wholly inclusive process of deliberation. This process is irrevocably debased beyond national frontiers by intergovernmentality. It will not do to argue that each of the leaders involved in the negotiations possesses national legitimacy: the sovereignty of a state cannot be conflated with that of a people. The state's external sovereignty is conceived on the model of game theory. This is the issue of freedom of choice in interacting with other states. For its part, popular sovereignty is the creation of the law guaranteeing equal liberties to all citizens. Procedures must therefore be identified for a transfer of sovereign rights to the supranational level that leaves national democratic procedures intact. More precisely, a way of formalizing in European law institutions capable of coordinating the relevant economic policies must be established in the eurozone, of a sort to banish the bureaucratic style of government that excludes citizens.

Habermas formulates three conditions for creating a democratic community. Today, they obtain only in nation-states: the free association of equal citizens assigning themselves rights that guarantee everyone's civic autonomy; a distribution of powers ensuring that collective decisions are indeed the fruit of the association of all citizens; and social inclusion through civic solidarity that supports the exercise of political authority. The first two conditions come under the organization of legal capacities that guarantee fundamental rights. The third concerns the sociocultural foundations of communication and debate in the political sphere. At a national level, government power is embedded in the grammar of the law, so that citizens exercise their authority through the law to which they submit. At a European level, this constitutional order does not exist – or not yet.

This is why the European Union is a curious hybrid. Unlike in a confederation of nations, there is a European law in the sphere of competition that takes precedence over national legislation; but, unlike in a federal state, there is no constitutional authority. That is why the priority of European law in areas where it obtains is not hierarchical. It is conceived as an alliance delegating limited powers to the Union. Once the latter has been recognized as having legal standing, European citizenship exists, but it is a weak form in terms of both political organization and social awareness.

It follows that the issue of shared sovereignty is still unresolved. The European Council is a legal anomaly. It may develop political orientations; but it can neither promulgate laws nor issue directives to the Commission. It can be a concentrated political authority in the event of a convergence of interests achieved through consensus; but it has no legal power to get them legitimated by citizens. At most, it can elicit institutional innovation through the simplified procedure of amending treaties.

As I will show in Chapters 8 and 9, it will be necessary to fashion the future, both to establish a social contract indispensable to an inclusive society and to accomplish the ecological transition, which is the basis for sustainable growth. This requires the political elites to win acceptance from the peoples of Europe through wide-ranging democratic debates. Sylvie Goulard and Mario Monti have correctly stressed the crucial importance of the inclusive role of democratic debate, conceived and organized so as to be directly European.[7]

8.

Can a New Social Contract be Established?

The European Community was initiated in the 1950s. It is commonly said that this was in order to prevent any return to war in Europe. This is true as regards relations between states. But what came out of the war was a profound transformation of European societies. In the six countries that formed the basis of the European Community, the same type of social contract developed, distinguishing them from the rest of the world, with the exception of the Scandinavian countries. The expansion of the wage-labour society, which emerged in the United States in the 1920s and was institutionalized by the New Deal, took a more finished form in Europe.

Universal social protection, labour law, trade-union recognition and collective bargaining are the social relations constitutive of the wage-labour society, which Pierre Rosanvallon prefers to call the 'redistributive society'.[1] It was a value common to all members of the European Community until the United Kingdom joined. These countries shared the same social contract. The values of solidarity distinguished them from Anglo-American political philosophy, as well as other types of society in the rest of the world.

The mutation of capitalism, which was rooted in the inflationary crisis of the 1970s and resulted in the financial crisis of the late 2000s, destroyed the European redistributive social contract. In the previous chapters, I have detailed the process of institutional transformation conducive to completing the euro. But the democratic legitimacy of these developments cannot be purely formal. It must be rooted in a genuine democracy, and that can only come from the development of a participatory social contract, in place of the defunct redistributive contract. Such a contract might, if one so wishes, be interpreted as a re-foundation of social democracy.

This chapter is devoted to advancing a number of ideas intended to prompt discussion of various features of such a social contract. It goes without saying that the French government's reorientation towards a 'contract of responsibility', in an attempt to pass on tax breaks to enterprises, has nothing to do with it.

As long as even 'advanced' societies remain organized around work, any social contract worthy of the name must be rooted in the enterprise. For this is the primary site of social inclusion. However, following thirty years of destruction of the principles formulated after the war, the enterprise has often become a site of discrimination, frustration, physical and intellectual exhaustion, and increasingly gigantic inequalities in the distribution of the product of labour. Destructive tendencies in the workplace fragment society and erode its cohesion, with negative consequences for the operation of democracy that are plain for all to see.

The first section of this chapter is therefore devoted to corporate governance. The wage-labour or redistributive society was based on managerial governance. The financial-ization of enterprises has destroyed it in favour of share-holder governance. A participatory social contract is compatible solely with partnership governance. What should the structures of coordination be? What about the distribution of powers? But also, what types of shareholders are consistent with partnership governance?

The second section concerns the principles social policy must adopt to be compatible with a participatory social contract. The main problem is the disproportionate infla-tion of financial rent, which shareholder governance has encouraged and helped to diversify in the form of capital gains and super dividends, extravagant managerial pay, inordinate pensions, and service charges paid to legal and financial elites. The basic issue is therefore the principles of social justice compatible with citizens' participation in the production of the public goods that make it possible to link the social contract to sustainable development.

Partnership Governance and Responsible Financial Investors

If the labour market were an ordinary market – determin-ing a correct price for labour, as claimed by the partisans of shareholder value to justify shareholders' monopoly on corporate power – there would be no need to develop labour law and specific ways of negotiating wages and conditions of labour. The labour market would function like a stock market. But labour is not exchanged. What is exchanged is the output of an independent worker's labour, or the hiring of a waged worker's labour-power for a given period of time. The wage is the monetary price of the hiring of labour-power for a given period of time. The work contract is therefore by its very nature incomplete, because labour-power is inalienable, except in a relationship of slavery. That is why its subordination is limited by a particular law – labour law – whereas ownership of an object pertains to civil law (*usus et abusus*).

The transformation of labour-power into a work flow is a process that has nothing to do with exchange by two equal parties in a competitive market. It is a relationship involving power on the part of the person in charge of performance of the work and subordination on the part of the person who performs it. Furthermore, there is nothing individual about this relationship. It involves complementarity and coordination in work collectives. There is an irreducible tension between these two aspects of cooperation and subordination. On the one hand, the enterprise is a team whose productivity depends on the cooperation and efficiency of its talents. It is therefore unrealistic to envisage separately measuring each employee's individual marginal contribution to the value produced by the enterprise and to have people believe that the wage structure expresses it. On the other hand, however, the enterprise as a human grouping is under the control of a private company that was conceived to achieve a capitalist objective: enhancement of the value of total corporate assets. It is not the ownership of a thing, but of a process of value-creation through the subordination of groups of human capacities.

It is therefore logical for this contractualization to respect collective rules negotiated between the employers and representatives of categories of wage-earners (collective bargaining). But such contractualization is necessarily incomplete, since subordination signifies that whoever commands the work of others has the right not to predetermine its content. This one-sidedness in the power relationship nevertheless has a quid pro quo, which can be demanded. Involved in creating value in a way that cannot be wholly contractualized, human capacities are intangible assets on top of their hiring costs. These intangible assets contribute to the enterprise's economic output. The wage-earners who are their bearers are stakeholders in total corporate value. They are partners in the enterprise, with whom it is right to make a social contract.

Why do we need such a contract? Because, in contrast to physical capital, the assets inherent in human persons are not recognized as property in corporate financial accounting. The latter does not treat them as capital. We can understand why enterprises run in accordance with shareholder value – i.e. enslaved to financial logic – do not treat them as stakeholders, unless what is involved is skills directly connected to financial management.

These theoretical considerations lead to the following result concerning corporate governance. An enterprise's intangible assets are specific by dint of their complementarity, which entails coordination capable of raising productivity, thereby increasing economic profitability. The form of governance capable of achieving this is a mechanism coordinating the multiple interests of stakeholders subject to the objective of maximizing the enterprise's total value. It is the role of the board of directors, as the corporate policy body, to determine shared strategic objectives, while abiding by the universal principle of valorization. Coordination mechanisms with strategic complementarities have multiple equilibria. There are therefore different models of governance, and we should not forget the possibility of failures of governance when the underlying relations change.

The social contract of the wage-labour society and its destruction by financialization

The dominant collective actor in the post-war wage-labour society was the large industrial enterprise. Finance was in a subordinate position because it was tightly regulated by the state, and above all because enterprises had the ability to finance themselves to a great extent. At the same time, the stock exchange was unimportant in continental Europe. General de Gaulle declared that France's policy was not made on the trading floor. The same was true of corporate strategy.

The large enterprise had a multifunctional, multi-divisional organization. It was able to internalize the conflicts arising from the subordination of labour in a techno-structure. Stakeholders' interests were managed by wage compromises negotiated between human resources departments and the trade-union representatives of categories of workers, in accordance with collective agreements lasting several years. The general principle guiding these compromises was indexation of nominal wages to inflation and indexation of real wages to productivity gains – generally sectoral, but sometimes involving the whole economy. In some countries, like France, where the public sector was large and powerful, collective public-sector negotiations set the norm for other economic sectors. The wages hierarchy in enterprises was managed on the basis of skills classification, determining stable pay scales and hence limiting internal conflicts.

So this was indeed a redistributive social contract. Through the intermediary of its trade-union representatives, the labour partner relinquished to the techno-structure, hence to corporate management, any say in production and investment that brought productivity gains. In return, management's objective was the long-term growth of the enterprise, which guaranteed the stability of the distributive compromise, making possible a general increase in income.

This social contract was therefore closely linked to managerial corporate governance, in which technical and human resources departments had the upper hand and financial departments pursued stable relations with banks for external inputs of finance to complement self-financing.

At a macroeconomic level, this mode of governance was formidably effective in maintaining high, non-volatile growth. This growth regime was at its height in the 1960s, developing the wage-labour society's mode of mass consumption based on urbanization, social housing, individual automobiles and domestic electrical equipment. The predictability of increasing demand fostered a high, regular rate of investment that incorporated productivity gains through industry's increasing output. Productivity rates supported rising real wages. Growth absorbed the young workforce emerging from the baby boom, maintaining a high level of employment.

The efficiency of this mode of regulation endured as long as productivity gains were sufficiently rapid to satisfy expectations of rising incomes. Yet advances in industrial productivity in mass production depended on continuous intensification of the division of labour and the pace of work. In the late 1960s, productivity growth began to slow under the impact, in particular, of workers' resistance to the intensification of work and conflicts within enterprises around young workers' resistance to the cumbersome hierarchies of managerial governance. As a result, rampant inflation set in, and fed off the celebrated wage-price spiral.[2]

Multiple shocks were grafted onto this process in the 1970s (American overheating, deliberately inflationary monetary policy under Nixon, the Vietnam War, destruction of the Bretton Woods system, oil shocks), transforming it into an inflationary crisis. This put an end to the mode of regulation of the wage-labour society in the late 1970s, when the chairman of the US Federal Reserve, Paul Volcker, decided to stamp out inflation by a radical switch in monetary policy. By massively increasing the cost of capital, this change put finance in command and systematically destroyed the wage-labour contract of managerial capitalism, promoting shareholder governance.

In Chapters 1–4, I highlighted the major features of this regime dominated by the financial cycle, and the reasons for its crisis. Here we may recall its effects on the wage-labour society in the countries that adopted it most fully. Its centre lay in the Anglo-American world, with the arrival in power of Ronald Reagan in the United States in 1980 and Margaret Thatcher in the UK in 1979. Its ideology is the ultra-liberalism that denies the specificity of labour, and therefore seeks to individualize the wage relationship to the maximum.

Finance's seizure of power in enterprises has resulted in the systematic destruction of trade-union power and the disappearance of the link between wage growth and productivity gains. At the same time, the rules that stabilized the wage hierarchy disappeared. Correspondingly, corporate organization was radically transformed through the outsourcing of tasks hitherto incorporated into the multifunctional enterprise, the razing of hierarchical structures with the disappearance of middle management, and the reorganization of enterprises into networks of autonomous profit centres controlled by the group's finance unit. From the mid 1980s, this change in structures prompted a wave of mergers, acquisitions, breakups and consolidations of firms, sparking the first euphoric enthusiasm of stock markets in the new era of financialized capitalism.

Huge changes in the division of labour generalized this enterprise model to most industrialized economies. The opening up of international trade to products manufactured by China and India expanded the global labour force enormously, creating a huge surplus in the supply of labour. The subsequent fall in unit wage costs in the emerging powers radically altered conditions of competitiveness in the industrialized countries, priming a twofold dynamic of relocation and ferocious pressure on wages and labour conditions. Simultaneously, the information revolution introduced a technological paradigm very different from the mechanization that guided the division of labour in the mass production of industrial goods. New qualifications emerged and others disappeared, reinforcing the tendency towards the individualization of wages and the polarisation of pay levels.

The macroeconomic consequences of these structural changes have been dramatic: a very marked slowdown – even complete stagnation in the Anglo-American countries – of median real wages; a rise in structural unemployment in Europe, especially France; and a race to the bottom on taxation of corporations and capital income, with chronic deficits in social budgets or the curtailment of rights in consequence.

A profound crisis in social cohesion has progressively set in. Intensification of the need for individual financial autonomy to compete in the lifestyle competition has come into conflict with pressure on the income of a majority of the population. Adjustment has occurred through general household debt – the main source of financial profit. The dynamic of the financial cycle has swept the whole growth regime off into systemic financial crisis.

The crisis of shareholder capitalism leaves behind a field of social ruin, whose full extent is not appreciated by governments. The intermediate institutions capable of working out collective compromises have lost much of their legitimacy. The loss of confidence in collective action has created endemic mistrust in the ability of politics to promote common goals. Social exclusion is experienced in broad swathes of society. Belief has taken root in a regression to a type of capitalism where the inclusion of labour is no longer on the agenda. And yet, it is from this crisis that we must derive the seeds of a revival of the social bond.

The need for a participatory social contract

There can be no way out of the crisis without a move to restore inclusive growth. This involves reconstructing a social contract with the ability to raise productivity. For, as we have seen on several occasions, labour productivity has stagnated and total factor productivity has fallen in the eurozone since 2007. The source of productivity gains lies in fostering work collectives.

In this respect, the digital revolution affords new opportunities. Technological tools (virtual platforms) bring together previously dispersed skills. Development takes the form of appreciation and recognition of collective human resources.[3] It is essential to regard them as an investment, and hence count them as such, in training and supporting managerial mobility and practice. The policies determining this investment are only effective if they are integrated into corporate strategic planning. The latter involves what is permanent about the enterprise, contrary to Wall Street, where nothing is permanent and everything must be amenable to liquidation in line with the vagaries of stock markets.

There is therefore a chain of intangible value deriving from the dynamic interdependence of individual intangible assets – for example, the role of tacit knowledge resulting from direct interaction between participants in an innovative investment project. Good-will innovation (quasi-profit) is generated by this synergy. Individuals with the associated skills are stakeholders in profits, and must participate in corporate governance. The peculiarity of the new technologies, and of the knowledge economy in general, is that they are based on wage-earners' interaction and involvement. Their motivation becomes the principal factor in productivity.

The integration of industry and services is an emerging technological field that opens up enormous possibilities for participatory forms of corporate organization. A collective intelligence is going to become increasingly indispensable for prevailing in competition. Consequently, wage-earners become stakeholders in the enterprise.[4] Because it mobilizes the human resources assembled in the enterprise, partnership governance is the main source of productivity.

Productivity essentially springs from collective learning: tacit knowledge via the circulation of skills that enhances individual abilities; informal interaction between employees in horizontal structures; motivation of wage-earners as partners. Only partnership governance through effective wage-earner participation on boards of directors can create the counter-powers required to ensure collective skills training as a factor of production.

The danger, obviously, is that the diversity in production due to multiplication of the services associated with material production will render relations between enterprises unstable. Such instability would impact upon employment. The answer is to be found in collaborative modes of production between suppliers and customers. It is also, and above all, to be found in the reallocation of workers to creative intelligence, which cannot be entrusted to computers. This is why the rise in labour costs is a major incentive to transform production processes. Automation reduces the need for unskilled labour and reinforces the need to invest in skills, to respond to demands for skilled labour.[5]

It follows that life-long education must become a fundamental right of citizenship, attached to the person, because it is indispensable to social inclusion. It must be publicly financed through a broadly based universal tax, and become a key concern of corporate strategies in partnership governance. This is precisely a participatory social contract. It must massively raise the population's general educational level, as the ability to interact depends above all on general skills.

Corporate social responsibility is therefore neither a little bit of soul nor a cost. What is at stake in partnership governance goes far beyond it, however, since intangible assets are not equivalent to physical capital. The latter depreciates with use. In addition, its accumulation with the same techniques entails a decline in its marginal productivity. By contrast, intangible capital improves with use. Its symbiosis with physical capital in processes that closely integrate material production and services counteracts the fall in the marginal productivity of corporate capital.

When enterprises are organized in networks that internalize externalities by dint of this interaction, they constitute innovation systems. To benefit from this coordination, a form of governance is needed that recognizes the diversity, interactive capacity and mobility of human skills – hence an extended partnership governance.

What kind of shareholders for partnership governance?

Challenging shareholder value goes hand-in-hand with abandoning every aspect of financialized capitalism. In Chapter 5, I advocated an intermediation that could finance the long term. Several systems are possible, but what they have in common is shareholder stability – unlike the principle of shareholder value, whereby the rotation of shareholders is a way of capturing short-term financial capital gains. By contrast, financial investors concerned with the long-term return on their investments are responsible investors.

A successful industrial ecosystem that practices partnership governance is the German *Mittelstand* (see Chapter 4). Naturally, it is not a question of copying the *Mittelstand*, but of noting that what we find there are responsible shareholders linked to partnership governance. More generally, responsible investors combine three concerns: service to the company in the sense of investment that bolsters inclusive, sustainable growth; the pursuit of long-term returns on the savings entrusted to them; and assessment of the social return on the productive investment that their financial input helps to realize. These concerns lead them into dialogue and negotiation with all the stakeholders concerned with investment plans, so as to internalize to the utmost the positive and negative externalities bound up with this investment. The idea is to calculate the total internal return on projects, taking account of future costs and benefits not assessed by the markets.

A long-term horizon is indispensable to such strategies. So are innovations in accountancy, because many of the social and environmental effects of the planned investment do not have a market price. Notional prices therefore have to be defined by debate among the stakeholders, making it possible to calculate their effects. This is possible for the purposes of internalizing externalities local to a town, a district, even a region. For general externalities like atmospheric pollution, the notional price of carbon must be established by the state – or, rather, by an agreement between states (see Chapter 9). We thus arrive at a formalization by partners of forms of interdependence presenting extended externalities.

The Principle of Justice and Social Choice

How can a sense of social belonging be deepened? The redistributive society developed a general solution: universal social protection. What were its regulatory effects?

Social protection to strengthen belonging

Growth is not a social end in itself. It is the economic process whereby the requirement of profit and capital accumulation can be reconciled with the exigencies of cohesion and progress in wage-labour societies. We have seen how managerial governance, closely linked to collective negotiation by social partners, contributed to it. But it is far from sufficient. For the same trend rate of growth can cover very different societies. Some are nightmares; others are cradles of human flourishing. Some secrete inequalities and forms of exclusion; others protect wage-earners from economic risks. Some are consumed by greed in the unbridled pursuit of individual enrichment; others deploy collective systems of solidarity.

It was to Europe's honour after the Second World War that it opted for the inclusion of citizens. The trauma of the war had made the political class in the belligerent countries understand that social solidarity was the cement of a community spirit. The choice of the last thirty years to develop the market, and nothing but the market, has destroyed this spirit. The possibility of a mode of regulation geared to social progress depends, above all, on political mediation.

After the Second World War, progress for everyone became the core value of social belonging. This value was written into programmes of education, social housing and social security. The capacity for economic regulation of the system of contributions and benefits was so effective that political parties adhered to it across the board. Consequently, social democracy imposed itself as a principle of affiliation. The principle of universal social protection is that no member of society should be left behind; all must be treated equally. This was not sheer rhetoric, unlike today's political speeches.

The stabilizing macroeconomic effect of social protection derived, in the first instance, from the fact that the indirect wage (as it was called) complemented collective negotiation by maintaining the regularity of wages over the economic cycle. This considerably cushioned the depth of the cycle. It comprised a set of social transfers (health services, unemployment benefit, minimum wage, progressive taxation) functioning as automatic stabilizers that significantly diminished the need for discretionary counter-cyclical fiscal policies. Disposable household income was thus uncoupled from fluctuations in primary income consequent upon unemployment. This preserved the evenness of final demand, and hence employment.

Obviously, models of social protection differed from one country to the next. But if we take the countries of continental Europe behind the European Union, the corporatist model based on labour was the one adopted, particularly in Germany and France. Its drawback, scarcely visible in the era of strong growth but very real, was that it concentrated the burden of social benefits on the shared contributions of employers and employees, and hence on wage costs. This created, and then aggravated, the dilemma of maintaining benefits or reducing the cost of financing them when, from the 1980s, growth fell. The social dialogue was irrevocably altered by this development.

Persistent discrimination against women: an enormous social cost

Despite its pretensions to universality, the system of redistribution ignored many forms of discrimination. Discrimination against women was not the least of them – involving, as it did, half of society. There is no doubt that the development of women's social roles has the greatest potential to transform societies for the better. It is also the sphere where the effects of growth are most impeded by majority mindsets frozen in stereotypes about social roles, in complete contrast to the radical alterations in production evoked above as catalysts of a participatory society. Finally, it is a terrain where political will can reconcile the social bond with individualistic aspirations and formal equality of citizenship, as has been done in Scandinavia.

From a purely quantitative point of view, the OECD has calculated what the equalization of male and female participation rates would generate in the way of additional growth over the period 2011–30, when compared with the inequality that prevailed in 2010. On average, the European Union would gain 0.5 per cent GDP growth per annum, Germany the same amount, France 0.4 per cent, Spain 0.6 per cent, and Italy 1 per cent. So this is far from insignificant, especially in an ageing continent.[6]

But this purely quantitative factor is too narrow a perspective, as forms of discrimination above all affect women's pay and job opportunities. With equal qualifications, and in the same areas of employment, the pay gap between men and women in France, which was 10 per cent in 2000, rose to 13 per cent in 2010 – contrary to the mistaken idea that things are spontaneously improving, slowly but surely. The gap increases as one advances up the pay scale. For the top 10 per cent of wages, it widens to 24 per cent. The gaps also grow with age, because of the career penalties imposed by employers using the pretext of maternity and attendant career breaks. Finally, inequalities are greater in countries where unionization rates are low.

The model of the nuclear, hierarchical family hailed from the United States, from the 1950s onwards. The household, not the individual, was the autonomous economic unit. The reason for this was a gender division of labour with a single monetary income, women being confined to family terrain. This total subordination of women could be presented in a progressive light. What was needed was a society that could deliver regular growth in the real income of its male wage-earning members, in order to maintain rising household incomes. It took expansion of the middle classes, along with universal education, for the lifestyle of the nuclear family to become the norm for the whole society. In a ruse of history, however, female education, an insatiable demand for labour and technological progress, with the development of the contraceptive pill, enabled the baby-boom generation to challenge the straitjacket in which it had lived. In the 1960s and '70s, women burst irrevocably onto the labour market. However, the advance of female labour was quantitatively uneven from country to country. Qualitatively, moreover, women always suffered from the obstacles of job

discrimination and the persistence of an utterly inegalitarian domestic division of labour.

Laws were passed establishing equal rights and equality
of opportunity in one country after another. But they did
not loom large in the mentality of employers, who were
simply able to ignore them in the absence of any serious
political will to implement them, except in Scandinavia.
Moreover, the labour market was highly segmented between
the sexes. The female workforce proved well-adapted to the
new growth regime. Highly flexible, accepting part-time,
low-wage jobs, women work in a much narrower range of
activities than men. Shops, office work, social services and
education account for more than 50 per cent of female
employment in the European Union. In jobs where women
are most numerous, wages tend to be low. Working in their
majority in casual jobs, on fixed-term contracts or via the
intermediary of temping agencies, they do not enjoy the
social protections attached to normal jobs.

The obstacles that maintain this state of affairs are deeply
encrusted in the structure of civil society, and inhabit the stereotypes in which a majority of the members of society, male or
female, represent social bonds to themselves. These obstacles
arise in the organization of enterprises and families alike.

A participatory society is one where all social functions are
shared equally. There is no reason in terms of efficiency –
quite the reverse – why senior management roles in enterprises should not be performed by as many women as men
overall in a country. But the enterprise culture establishes
rites of passage for promotion to positions of power. A significant rite for cadres who are candidates for senior promotion
– a rite that has nothing to do with efficiency, but everything

to do with probation – is demonstrating a willingness to work a ridiculous number of hours per week and to be instantly available to travel anywhere in the world. Boxed in by the irreducible rigidity of family chores, most married women cannot meet these requirements. Add to this the firmly rooted caste prejudices of senior directors in large enterprises, finance and the civil service regarding the supposed emotionalism of the 'female temperament', and one will have an idea of the mechanisms of social segregation.

The social lock is also based on extreme inequality in the domestic division of labour. All investigations indicate that domestic labour, care, and time devoted to children are very unequally shared, even when both wife and husband work full-time. Certainly, the degree of inequality varies from one country to another, and decreases among young couples. This may be an encouraging sign of a future change in attitudes. At all events, confronted with the contradictory exigencies of company and family, women no longer leave the labour market, but resign themselves to a status that excludes them from social promotion.

Equality of opportunity is a principle of fairness in a participatory society. Well-meaning souls, of whom there are many among economists, shamelessly invoke it while 'forgetting' that the principle is not applied to half the population. A society emancipated from personal subordination would enjoy economic advantages in terms of supply and demand, over and above the purely quantitative aspect of increased employment calculated above. The unit of consumption would no longer be the nuclear family, but the individual in an equal, two-career family. Diversity of consumption would be greatly enhanced, especially in services.

The most important gain would consist in productive supply. Female and male educational levels have attained parity. If the artificial locks shutting women out of the social positions to which they are legally entitled were broken, they would no longer be confined to narrow segments of the division of labour. The supply of skilled labour would be diversified and significantly expanded, to the advantage of enterprises. On the assumption that women bring a different approach to professional problems, and to participation in group work that values cohesion over competition, the organizational flexibility of enterprises would be enhanced. Leadership styles would be augmented, and the capacity for innovation could be increased.

To advance in this direction, we need changes in practices in civil society and institutional reforms. Gender stereotypes must be eliminated as early as primary school. Recognition of the value of gender equality must be enforced in place of the subordination of women. It is also necessary to invest in public goods and services so that everyday life and professional careers will become compatible. Subsidized, high-quality services, complemented by maternity leave and parental leave and preserving the position of people (men or women) in enterprises, would make it possible for women to pursue careers while maintaining fertility rates that guarantee the reproduction of generations. Finally, and especially, as the Scandinavian experience has shown, it will be necessary to pass through a period of positive discrimination, with quotas for positions of power, so as to smash, once and for all, the social obscurantism that perpetuates forms of negative discrimination.

Which principles of justice for a participatory society?

The requirement of fairness signifies a concern for the other, as opposed to the utilitarian postulate of ultra-liberalism. In fact, since Arrow's proof of the impossibility theorem, we have known that there is no procedure for social choice capable of satisfying individual preferences that can be characterized as rational and democratic.[7] According to Rawls, fairness is, in the first instance, everyone's equal right to a set of real (not merely formal) basic freedoms, which he calls primary goods.[8] The legitimate inequalities compatible with fairness must satisfy two conditions. The first is that all social positions be open to everyone, and hence that mechanisms of exclusion and discrimination be abolished. The second is that inequalities in position, whenever justified, be conducive to social efficiency, in the sense that the greatest benefits accrue to the most disadvantaged members of society.

The transformation of financialized capitalist society, which is a machine for producing exclusion, into a participatory society therefore takes the form above all of eliminating the vicious circles that block any possibility of upward social mobility. They are obstacles that impair people's ability to exercise their real freedoms – that is, to transform their 'capabilities', in Amartya Sen's sense, into viable life plans.[9]

The elimination of poverty traps, defined as the deprivation of primary goods, must be the pole star of public policies for inclusion. It is enough to observe the results of French housing and education policy to see how far removed we are from this. Over and above that minimum objective, there is no principle of social justice that could be unanimously characterized as optimal or superior. Social choice is a sphere of developing policies for relative improvements. By means of deliberation and common agreement in a participatory society, we must be able to pronounce situations that are increasingly frequent in 'advanced' societies unjust – for example, the recurrent financial manipulation and deliberate collusion that prevail in the international banking lobby, inordinate income inequalities, forms of job discrimination, exclusion from access to healthcare, organized tax evasion.

For democracy to advance society in the direction of participation, it must be indissolubly linked to the requirement of fairness. It must range considerably beyond electoral procedures, organizing citizens' intervention in debates about concrete social policy. This involves a much more demanding dissemination of information than is accomplished by the media and a multiplicity of sites of counter-power developing reasoned positions. Public debate can change attitudes to gender discrimination. But improvement in the quality of public debate entails efforts to raise general educational levels. Such is the sense of the democratic order. Such should be the logic of the *Rechtsstaat*.

What Form Would a Sustainable Growth Regime Compatible with the Ecological Transition Take?

For a growth regime to meet the challenges of the twenty-first century, it will have to be not only inclusive but also sustainable. Like the rest of the world, Europe is experiencing a triple crisis – financial, social and ecological. The first two have been studied in the preceding pages. The third is evolving more slowly because of the inertia in the interaction between environment and economy. But this dimension of the crisis possesses the greatest destructive potential. Conversely, making the ecological transition the guiding principle of a pro-growth policy would have beneficial effects on the other two dimensions. As we shall see, it would make it possible to revitalize genuine democracy, involving social choices ranging from the international political arena to local areas. This also requires a transformation of finance in the direction spelled out at the end of Chapter 5: the encouragement of responsible long-term investors.

Sustainable growth, which some people call sustainable development, must first be defined, so that the principle guiding long-term policies is clear. The energy transition in the broad sense, undertaken in the light of climate change – that is, encompassing the energy efficiency of the totality of production processes, transport and housing – will require long-term investment that can restore growth and alter its quality. The malfunctions occasioned by the contradictory options of Germany and France indicate just how indispensable a European energy policy is. However, financing this transition requires financial intermediation bound up with a social value for carbon, very different from the financialization of the past three decades. This is an additional reason for radically restructuring finance. Finally, energy efficiency involves refashioning the productive system in the direction of the circular, territorialized economy. This would help to enhance the integration of industry and services and to reshape areas that have suffered deindustrialization.

Social Well-Being and the Quality of Growth

An economic policy geared to social well-being must be orientated by very different reference points, measures and resources from those that currently obtain. National accounting organized around gross domestic product (GDP) should be profoundly altered in the direction explored by the UN panel of experts on inclusive wealth.[1]

GDP, which is still regarded by governments as the ultimate criterion of policy success or failure, is an essentially market-value stream over a given period. It erases the problems of allocation to which I referred in Chapter 8. The same level of GDP can be achieved in highly inegalitarian societies, and in societies that have constructed effective systems of collective protection against social risks and of income redistribution via taxation. Is it right to say that these societies enjoy the same level of social well-being?

Let us take the United States, which has an average per capita monetary income higher than that of most European countries. Is this a good measure of well-being, indicating that the United States is a more developed society than Europe? To a considerable extent, high average wages compensate for the highest health costs in the world, because there is no social system of health insurance in the private sector, despite the timid, abortive reform by Barack Obama, and because the collusion between the health professions and private insurance companies keeps health service prices exorbitantly high. Furthermore, the dizzying rise in inequalities excludes around 47 million Americans from any health insurance. All this cannot be read in the GDP. On the contrary, GDP is inflated by the high wages required to pay for the profit extracted by the health professions and insurance companies. Finally, if we examine the direct health performance indicators calculated by the World Health Organization (WHO), the United States is among the lowest performers among advanced countries when it comes to life expectancy and indicators of morbidity, including heart disease and obesity.

Let us now consider the major oil producers: Nigeria, Russia, Saudi Arabia and Venezuela. According to the UN's assessment criteria, none of these countries is on a sustainable path as regards the inclusive wealth indicator. This means they are incapable of reinvesting the income derived from fossil resources extracted below ground into factors of wealth generating social well-being for their populations.

These countries are destroying their wealth, and thus reducing the well-being of future generations. However, their GDP is growing.

These observations and many others indicate that neither the natural capital furnished by ecosystems, nor the social capital furnished by people in and through collaboration, are counted as capital either by nations or by enterprises, since they do not have privately appropriable property rights or a market price as assets. It follows that a purely market logic cannot claim to be conducive to a social optimum, any more than economic policies directed exclusively at regulating the path of GDP can.

In 2008, a commission on measuring economic performance and social progress was established under the chairmanship of Joseph Stiglitz. Its report, delivered in September 2009, proposed various ways of overcoming the aporias of existing accounting systems: enriching GDP by taking account of social inequalities in an adjusted assessment; complementing GDP with indicators that would make it possible for governments to pursue binding objectives; and, finally, extending accounting to the measurement of categories of capital ignored in the standard system, by drawing up satellite accounts with a view to a future system that comprises a general conception of capital.[2] None of these approaches was considered by any government, apart from Norway's, to guide the strategy of its sovereign fund. On the other hand, some enterprises, taking their social responsibility seriously, and some responsible institutional investors, did take an interest.

The UN method is the most complete because it seeks to assess the marginal social contributions to well-being of the various components of general capital, and hence to measure what the market does not, because the costs and benefits of these various assets are externalities – that is, influences ignored by markets.

Such marginal contributions to social well-being are controversial, because they are 'shadow prices' whose assessment can stem not only from a debate between stakeholders concerned by the harmful consequences of pollution and the destruction of soil fertility, but also a climate of social conflict and a skills shortage. To forge tools for measuring sustainable growth is therefore to advance real democracy. It is also to give it a long-term dimension, since society is a collective that endures over time. Well-being is trans-generational; its productive basis is the nation's total wealth, encompassing all forms of capital. A nation's net investment in the frame of reference of sustainable growth is the rate at which total social wealth progresses, when the different assets that make up this wealth are measured in the light of their marginal contribution to social well-being over a period for which these contributions may be taken as constant. Growth is sustainable over a period in which this condition is confirmed if net investment, thus measured, does not decrease.

Measurement of the wealth of nations employing this methodology is still out of reach, and will remain so as long as governments have not made arrangements to develop their statistical systems in such a way as to expand the measurement of capital and integrate it into a revised accounting system.[3] On the basis of theoretical results bearing on the quality of growth, however, it is already possible to define investment priorities for the purposes of sustainability.

The rationale offered for changing nothing in the habitual frame of reference of growth, and hence not altering our conception of government action, is invariably the same: belief in market fundamentalism. If one thinks that different forms of capital can be substituted for one another, then one believes that it is always possible in the existing accounting and hence price system to substitute forms of capital that can be produced (machines, equipment, information systems) for forms of capital that cannot be produced (reconstitution of ecosystems), or which are allowed to be deliberately destroyed (deforestation, acidification and exhaustion of ocean resources). If, on the contrary, substitutability of forms of capital is low or zero, the destruction of forms of capital that are not reproduced threatens the long-term sustainability of societies as a whole.

There are at least two kinds of destructive development of natural capital that cannot be subject to substitution by existing capital in the current modes of allocation of economic activities. These are loss of biodiversity and climate change. Biodiversity does not readily lend itself to general valorization. It involves localized, targeted policies on the basis of specific indicators and binding norms. By contrast, climate change, which is the cause of a general externality, can be addressed with the aid of a universal standard price: the social value of carbon. Investment in controlling climate change has the potential to profoundly renew the growth regime in the direction of sustainable development.

The Energy Transition at Risk from Climate Change

The energy transition, related to climate change and not merely future scarcity of sources of fossil energy, is not simply a process of substitution of renewable energy resources for non-renewable ones. It is a comprehensive transformation of production in the direction of energy efficiency, with which carbon efficiency is closely correlated. In this sense, it may be characterized as a secular wave of innovation.

Secular innovations foster the accumulation of capital over long periods because they radically transform social existence. The combined development of change in economic structures and in social institutions inflects growth paths over very long periods. Part and parcel of capitalist logic, such radical innovations are embodied in structures of production and in ways of life by the wagers of finance. Crises of adaptation are therefore always marked by large-scale financial crises resulting from excess in the valuation of the promises of profitability spawned by these innovations. In and through these financial crises, the growth regime is redefined. Major waves of innovation can overlap, with the crisis of adaptation of one type of innovation coexisting with the emergence of the next. Thus, the Taylorist organization of work developed in the integrated production lines of heavy industry spread to the mass production of durable consumer goods, spearhead of the following wave of innovations.

Cross-checking information on the dates of industrial revolutions and the onset of major financial crises, and then on studies of the so-called Fordist era, we can compile Table 9.1, complemented by fragmentary knowledge about the ongoing revolutions in information technology and the environment.

Table 9.1: Secular Innovations

Type of innovation	Emergence	Diffusion	Crisis of adaptation	Maturity	Total period
Steam engine and textiles	1762-1774	1794-1834	1834-1843	1844-1861	1762-1861
Rail and iron and steel	1831-1847	1847-1888	1888-1895	1896-1917	1831-1917
Mass production	1882-1908	1908-1937	1937-1949	1950-1973	1882-1973
Information and communication	1961-1981	1981-2000	2000-2013	2013- ?	1961- ?
Environment	1972-2015	2015- ?	??	??	1972- ?

Sources: Joseph Schumpeter (*Business Cycles*, 1939), David Landes (*The Unbound Prometheus*, 1969), and Michel Aglietta (*A Theory of Capitalist Regulation*, 1976)

It describes the roll-out of innovations that have punctuated the historical epochs of capitalism since the first Industrial Revolution. They range far beyond economic policies, involving the whole society of the countries they transform, either directly or through the repercussions of labour mobility on more traditional sectors. However, these innovations require complementary public and private investment. Thus, the automobile completely reshaped cities. They unfold in successive phases (Table 9.1). Structural investment plays a major role in their expansion, because it involves investment streams that realize the paradigm of the major innovation in the whole economy. It is the link between the generic innovation revolutionizing technological progress and transforming a way of life and the incremental innovation concretely realizing it in enterprises.

The possibility of a wave of radical innovations based on the environment is not universally recognized. If we date the inaugural event to the Club of Rome's warnings in 1972, it took a very long time to emerge. Even the Rio Earth Summit in 1992, and subsequent international conferences, did not really launch the dissemination phase. That occurs when the principle containing the relevant secular innovation becomes dominant in investment decisions taken by countries that are leaders in the technologies that materially embody this innovation. Even if ever more economic actors and governments are persuaded of the reality of climate change and its human origin, the financial link triggering the massive investment of the start of the dissemination phase has yet to be made.

My hypothesis is that Europe has an opportunity to seize, and that the inaugural moment happened with the 2015 Paris conference, called COP21, that sealed the Paris Accord. If Europe grasps the opportunity to be the pioneer in an industrial revolution that is going to transform the technological frontier, it can generate a strong revival in growth and play a prominent role in future international negotiations. The European countries also have to cooperate on an integrated energy policy. The unilateral choice of the German energy transition, on the one hand, and the French government's inaction in the face of the nuclear lobby, on the other, have hitherto rendered such cooperation impossible.

Setbacks in the German energy transition
and its consequences for Europe

In principle, Germany has fully embarked on environmental secular innovation: a proactive fall in greenhouse gas (GHG) emissions of 40 per cent between now and 2020 compared with 1990, and the abandonment of nuclear in 2022. But the transfers involved in financing the cost of the transition have not been fairly shared, and have accentuated inequalities. The dual objective of sustainable development – inclusion and sustainability – has not been met.[4]

The first paradox is the renewed rise in GHG since 2011, on account of the increase in the share of carbon-based energy production, itself due to the development of shale gas in the United States. At the same time, efforts to improve energy efficiency have slowed, because the pace of building renovation is well below target. On the other hand, renewable energies are developing thanks to subsidies. But the cost of these subsidies is borne by households and SMEs. This disadvantages the poorest households. Large industrial enterprises, by contrast, benefit from exemptions. For the bill for investment in the production of renewable energy is large (€120 billion for 2005–12). As regards housing renovation, even if the programme has recently reached its ceiling in sums invested, it is far in excess of the French performance: 165,000 housing units per annum for €76,000 per unit, as against 50,000 units for €37,000 per unit in France over 2005–12.

The future costs of strengthening electricity distribution networks and increasing storage capacity, and the ability to rebalance between energy sources, are high, but indispensable to the stability of the electricity system because of the growing importance of intermittent energy sources. Earlier exit from nuclear than initially planned is creating an additional cost for dismantling the reactors and managing waste that is difficult to assess.

Transfers to finance renewables and subsidize enterprises that are major energy consumers are high. The upshot is discrimination in electricity prices. Large industrial consumers of electricity pay prices equivalent to French prices, while other consumers pay 40–90 per cent more. The market prices of primary energy sources are completely dysfunctional relative to the needs of a 'low-carbon' economy. The development of shale gas in the US unlocks coal-fired reactors producing for Europe, rather than closing them, especially given that the price of CO_2 is at rock bottom. However, final prices for retail consumers are not falling.

While adaptation through building renovation, courtesy of financing by the KfW bank, boasts a positive balance sheet, especially given that it is a good way of supporting economic activity and creating jobs, CO_2 reduction through support for renewable energies has temporarily stalled. This is a profound malfunction, because gas-fired reactors have been halted while coal-fired reactors burning lignite (the most polluting) have replaced them. The causes are the same throughout Europe, and stem from developments in world prices: a doubling of gas prices between 2005 and 2012 and a fall of 40 per cent in coal prices between 2011 and 2013. To counteract it, a CO_2 price of the order of €50 per metric ton avoided would be required, and hence a genuinely integrated European energy and climate change policy. Aside from progress on buildings, the transport lobby is blocking any decrease in car emissions, as a result of which emissions have not fallen in the industry for four years.

Pursuing the energy transition in one country comes up against the integration of European energy markets as regards networks and regulations. Greater cooperation is not an option, but a necessity. It does not mean all countries making the same choices about the composition of primary energies for electricity production. But it does mean investment in an intelligent storage and distribution network unified at a European level. This requires technological partnerships for networks and renewable energies, so that solar is developed in Greece rather than on the shores of the Baltic. To achieve it, long-term strategic planning to decide common objectives is imperative. This directly raises the issue of the massive long-term finance that existing intermediation systems – commercial banks and capital markets – are incapable of taking on.

Financing the energy transition
for sustainable growth in Europe

The investment demanded by the climate challenge does not come under business as usual. It suffers from a dual uncertainty, ecological and technological, and consequently presents risks that are not easy to grasp, because they are non-financial risks resulting from externalities not evaluated by the market. It pertains to very cumbersome structures that are affected by considerable irreversibilities. These require extended, hefty financing, while any returns on investment lie in the distant future.

For all these reasons, capital markets provide highly inadequate finance, as we can see in observing the limited attractiveness of 'green' bonds. Institutional investors hold shares and bonds that are readily negotiable, and these do not include debt securities financing infrastructure and the environment. The latter are alternative assets that institutional investors virtually do not hold (less than 1 per cent of their portfolio in the case of the pension funds of OECD countries).[5] As for banks, they are not equipped to tie up loans over the long term if they cannot share the risks, and hence find investors capable of long-term commitments. In short, the transition will be too slow if the European states do not organize the requisite industrial policy and the financial intermediation capable of supporting it.

Up until now, nothing has happened. Thus, energy policies in Europe are chaotic and contradictory, as we have just noted in connection with the German energy transition. In the absence of any consistency in the policies pursued by different countries, subsidies for new energy sources can be excessive, and then vanish abruptly, with devastating effects on the cash flow of current projects. From the standpoint of sources of finance, pronounced diversification of instruments and a change of scale are indispensable.

Political uncertainty and the unfitness of financial markets to invest in environmental infrastructure represent a dual handicap. The obstacles to alternative investment are well-known: the competition among asset managers to achieve quarterly records serves only to promote short-term returns; most investors have regulatory restrictions on holding long-term assets; the competition policy that separates network producers and service providers forces investors to choose the property rights they wish to hold, without being able to build synergies into their investment, whereas the activities are technically and economically integrated. There is little price history and no benchmark, forcing complete internalization of the management of these assets, which is costly. Green investors suffer additional handicaps. The most crippling is the nonexistence or inadequacy of a carbon price determined on the pollution permits (cap-and-trade) market. This handicap is all the more prohibitive in that innovations in low-carbon investment carry both technological and ecological risks. In the absence of credible valuation of carbon, guaranteed by governments and growing over time, and without a halt to subsidies for fossil fuels, such investment is dominated by existing infrastructure.

To redirect savings into low-carbon investment, it is necessary to reduce the risk profiles of projects for investors, without overburdening tax-payers. To that end, a reduction in emissions has to have an increasing monetary value over time. But this monetary value cannot at present be provided by a tax or a market focused on current transactions, which economies gravely weakened by the crisis would not be able to support.[6] We must therefore think differently. The financial basis for the transition to a low-carbon economy can only be monetary.

Proposal for the monetary financing of carbon assets

To embark upon the growth regime of the twenty-first century, it has become imperative to redeploy investment far beyond the energy sector: transport, construction, new materials and their transformation, recycling of waste and bio-agriculture. To identify the finance requirements, two notions must be distinguished: on the one hand, the payment stream over the whole term of an investment, which must be covered by the income generated so as to yield investors an internal rate of return higher than the cost of the capital (a weighted average of the market return on shares and long-term debt securities); on the other, the sum to be advanced for constructing equipment, experimenting in the production processes, and market research before commercialization generates the initial cash flow (upfront costs). There is therefore a dual problem to be overcome. Investment in emissions reduction has a social return (for the collectivity), one aspect of which is a reduction in the quantity of GHG in the atmosphere. This involves a positive externality through reduction of a negative externality. If it is not recognized by a price, calculation of the investment's internal rate of return will be undervalued, and the investment project will be dominated by the pursuit of investment (in energy, for example) that is more polluting. It must be possible to calculate a full internal rate of return that builds the social gain of the carbon reduction into future cash flows. What is therefore required is a sufficiently high valuation of carbon to trigger a stream of investment in emissions reduction, which has become imperative. Furthermore, investment in the climate transition has a high start-up and set-up cost, because the cash-flow returns only cover these costs at the end of the cycle.

This distinction coincides with one that must be made between net and gross volume of investment. The volume of gross investment is very high, but the volume of long-term net investment in low-carbon technologies can be low, because the gross costs will be offset, if all goes well, by a massive decrease in demand for energy bound up with greater efficiency and, above all, the gains deriving from technological options and urban consumption patterns that are more fuel-efficient thanks to adaptation ('smart cities').

The first innovation needed to initiate a low-carbon investment stream is political. It falls to the Council of the heads of state of the European Union, and it consists in establishing a social value for carbon throughout Europe. This will be neither a price determined in a carbon market, nor a tax built into the price of current commodities. It is a notional price defined as the value of a metric ton of CO_2-equivalent avoided, and is applied to new investments and not already established capital. It has the same logical significance as the discount rate. Moreover, it is indispensable to counter-balance the obstacle represented by the discount rate to calculating the projected profit of long-term, risky projects.

This proposal introduces a temporal distinction into climate policy by distinguishing between the valuation of new investments – future capital to be generated – and of already established capital and the goods and services it produces. This distinction is made because investment is long-term and uncertain, while the establishment of a tax or market price at a sufficient level to make such investment possible is currently not politically feasible in most countries. It is the realization of low-carbon investments that will progressively alter the structure of production and make a carbon tax possible and acceptable.

The social value of carbon, defined in monetary units, establishes a new space of commensurability – that of carbon assets. These are values applied to the volumes of CO_2-equivalents avoided by low-carbon investment in all economic activities. They are joint products of all low-carbon–orientated investments, whether for reduction or adaptation, whether centralized or decentralized. There is a carbon asset when the quantity of greenhouse gas avoided by an investment has been confirmed and certified by independent expert agencies.

To launch an effective European investment policy on the basis of the valuation of carbon assets, the governments of member-states must commit to guaranteeing a certain quantity of carbon assets for a period of five years. This commitment would be subject to an agreement sealed by the European Council and validated by the European Parliament. For enterprises with plans, the advantage lies in the certainty of an increase in the social value of carbon over time, which raises the value of long-term investment compatible with climate policy relative to other investment. For lenders seeking to reduce the losses contained in assets inherited from the crisis, and accumulating liquidity, this is an opportunity for sources of credit whose risk is shared on a par with the validated carbon assets. The system of financial intermediation that delivers such risk-sharing remains to be determined.[7]

Its pivot is the ECB. Thanks to government guarantees on the carbon assets produced by investments, the Central Bank can include the value of the guaranteed carbon assets in the assets on its balance-sheet. In return, it would issue carbon certificates on its liabilities. These would join the reserves of financial bodies (investment banks, development banks, investment funds) that have financed investment plans validated by the certification agencies. Uncertainty for the risk-takers who finance the projects, deriving from the upfront costs of the financed projects, is in a sense partly socialized. It is reduced by the sum of carbon certificates out of the guaranteed carbon assets. As for the Central Bank, this kind of monetary activity may be regarded as forming part of the policy of quantitative easing implemented since the crisis. The difference is that, unlike the purchase of government or mortgage securities that monetize existing debts, the monetary financing of carbon assets applies to the creation of new real assets. These assets are values produced by investment that would not be undertaken without the risk-sharing.

The kind of finance proposed corresponds to a transitional monetary policy, like the quantitative action by central banks in response to the financial crisis. Exit from it can be envisaged when low-carbon investment has demonstrated its efficiency by significantly reducing GHG concentration and equipping economic agents to adapt more effectively to climate change. The condition for exit from monetary finance is eventual convergence between the valuation of the carbon externality through financial tools and the valuation that would derive from a future carbon tax. This convergence condition ensures the temporal coherence of the hoped-for return on investments. For a flexible exit from the financial policy of carbon asset purchases, the Central Bank could simply no longer acquire them in exchange for the carbon certificates presented by the banks (a kind of tapering), but conserve the stock on its balance sheet. It could also progressively return them to the market in the form of green bonds, destroying the previously created counterpart money.

Decentralization: Towards a Circular and Territorial Economy

Climate change is not the only threat to the growth regime of capitalist economies. According to the definition of sustainable growth offered at the beginning of this chapter, it is the preservation of the total social wealth of nations that is at stake. As intimated in the Club of Rome's conclusions, the super-exploitation of ecosystems and finite natural resources cannot be self-regulating, for it is ignored by the norms that finance posts to guide investment. There is no 'fundamental value' revealed by financial markets in the case of non-produced assets, bearers of absolute scarcity, whether renewable or not.

The tendency for the real price of raw materials other than petrol to fall over the twentieth century (70 per cent on average) was reversed in the opening decade of the twenty-first century. The upshot has been financial imbalances and social disorder exacerbated by financial speculation. The logic of capital accumulation in conditions of competition has spurred a relentless increase in the productivity of labour and physical capital. Nothing of the sort has occurred in the case of natural capital. If prices fell over a long period, it is because the social cost of reproducing renewable resources (forests, water and fisheries), on the one hand, and the cost of the exhaustion of non-renewable resources, on the other, were not fully taken into account. This was not because technologies were selected to increase the productivity of natural resource usage. On the contrary, wastage, the increase in waste products, water pollution and the destruction of species by chemical products, the exhaustion of soil by intensive agriculture – these are persistent characteristics of capitalist modes of production and consumption.

The circular economy based on recycling is the first step in transforming productive systems to enhance efficient use of resources.[8] Public authorities are beginning to move to make producers responsible for managing the waste deriving from their production processes. The issue remains the same. Protocols and regulations must be created to induce economic agents to internalize environmental externalities in place of defective markets. The economies could be enormous. For example, producing glass from sand consumes five times more energy than producing it from recycled glass. According to a report from the UN Environment Programme, the recycling of metals is far below potential re-use. There are numerous sources of economies: lower extraction costs, lower energy and water expenditure, less degradation of the natural environment, and lower CO_2 emissions.

For Europe, the circular economy could be a vehicle of industrial competitiveness and local restructuring of economic activities in the cause of sustainable growth. The circular economy re-territorializes the activities of production, unlike linear value chains; what is a residue for one activity becomes a resource for another, in exchange loops. Seeking to increase the productivity of raw-material usage, the circular economy is a principle for integrating ecology and economics. To implement this principle, recycling must be envisaged from the moment products are conceived. It is therefore a logic of innovation that seeks to benefit from positive externalities in a general model of viable development. Unlike the mechanical conception of economic growth in neoclassical theory, the circular economy orientates economic development towards the theory of complex systems: the importance of feedback loops, multi-functionality, saturation of sub-systems' capacity for repair, and hence limits to recycling.

Given the forms of inter-dependency involved, the political actors in the front line are local political authorities. It falls to them to organize local democracy to produce a strategic collective intelligence that makes it possible to create a cooperative network of local collectivities, associations of citizens and enterprises to foster bottom-up innovation. Continuously developing, open information systems are needed to assess local policies.[9] This means deepening democracy. From the European level, establishing the social value of carbon, to the organization of real democracy and enterprise networking locally, European governance must become multi-level and multi-agent in order to fashion the future.

What Is Europe's Role in the New Age of Globalization?

Europe as such does not exist politically. The first reason, underscored throughout this book, is the incompletion of the euro. Europe will only have political influence if the institutional developments discussed in Chapters 5–7 are implemented. A European constitutional order, legitimating political power at community level, is a precondition for articulating a European goal for the world.

But that is not enough. This ambition must also be relevant, offering answers to the problems humanity will face in this century. As I have recalled, after the Second World War such an ambition existed. It was to establish peace and offer the world the most advanced model of social progress. In our era, as I tried to show in Chapters 8 and 9, inclusive, sustainable growth should be the goal.

This poses a serious problem, because that ambition is not expressed in influential political circles in Europe, other than in campaign speeches or media posturing. It is not adopted by governments in their domestic policy, whose alpha and omega is fiscal austerity. How could it be projected externally? But there is a deeper ideological problem. For more than thirty years, Europe has abandoned the social-market economy for market fundamentalism. The logical consequence has been unilateral political alignment with the United States, the sole exception being France and Germany's non-participation in the disaster of the second Iraq War. Enlargement of the European Union was conducted in line exclusively with Anglo-American attitudes, a constant of which is hostility to Russia. The political disruptions in 2016 and 2017 have changed that landscape. On the other hand, Brexit, the election of Donald Trump and his rebuttal of the US hegemonic world order have been wake-up calls for the EU to assert itself as a political power in world politics. Meanwhile the rise to power of enormous continental nations in Asia, which are not in the Western orbit and are not wedded to market fundamentalism, should give us pause for thought about the possibility and meaning of pursuing radical financial globalization in a space of nations with contradictory interests in the absence of global governance.

Let there be no misunderstanding of the true significance of the string of financial crises from the mid 1990s to the general crisis of 2007–08. It means that general market multilateralism cannot exist in the absence of the production of general public goods capable of constituting global regulation. In current conditions, globalization can only recede, as it has done several times in the history of capitalism: in the seventeenth century, following the Renaissance expansion; in the first decades of the nineteenth century, after the age of the Enlightenment and the collapse of Napoleonic imperialism; in the years 1914–58, following the major financial expansion of the 1873–1913 period. A multilateralism that is limited in order to be viable is a reasonable prospect for the post-crisis period we are now in.[1]

However, a new phenomenon confronts every nation in this century. The ebbs and flows of world capitalism have revealed the impossibility of self-regulation exclusively by market logic. The essence of capitalism is boundless expansion, spreading inequality and conflict. It comes into collision with the fragmentation of national spaces. The contradiction was overcome by the assertion of a military and monetary hegemony which, for a time, organized capital accumulation, leading to growth that was shared to some degree. Furthermore, hegemony did not elude the Western world in the lands ploughed up by capitalism during its geographical expansion. But hegemony always ends up declining, smothered by the costs it entails. Trump's rhetoric continuously emphasizes those costs to retreat from international responsibilities to 'make America great again'.

A hypothesis worth exploring is that the twenty-first century will not accord with past developments. Asian capitalism is not a pupil of market fundamentalism. Chinese economic power has become a fact of life. It is the structural pole of trade in East Asia. The political aim is to make China the focal point of an integrated regional space, to project its enterprises to absorb technology, to secure access routes to resources and multiply long-term partnership agreements with states on the African and South American continents. This is a conception of international relationships that is not multilateral from the outset in and through a world market. It advocates organizing regional spaces and multilateralism through a form of governance constructed out of the need to collaborate in producing general public goods.

Forming a space that would be consolidated by the euro's completion by 2020, and which would have a power of attraction over neighbouring North Africa and the Middle East, Europe could be a mediator in establishing such governance, if it can recover a desire for political autonomy. The two kinds of general public goods for which global governance should be negotiated are climate change and the international monetary system. Moreover, they are linked, since establishing a notional value for carbon and monetary financing of carbon assets, the necessity of which I noted in Chapter 9, must be accessible to all countries.

International Climate Negotiations

The major problem rendering climate negotiations so difficult is that man-made climate change is a general threat to the whole of humanity, but responsibility for it and the potential consequences are, and will remain, unequal. Climate change represents a general externality. Its historical causes are very unequally distributed between countries, depending on when they joined in the industrial revolution, and especially on their massive utilization of carbon energies.

It is also a general externality whose effects are regionally differentiated, on account of the geographical characteristics peculiar to climate change and the characteristics peculiar to the economies that do and will endure it, and whose resilience to this kind of shock varies greatly. The first victims of the effects of climate change will be the least advanced countries, island states, and the disadvantaged populations of emerging countries. Finally, this general externality has significant effects on future generations, by dint of the time constants specific to the physical laws of accumulation of carbon sinks and the particularly long lifespan of certain GHGs.

Climate policy, which requires the allocation of public resources, intersects with societal goals regarding human health, food security, biodiversity, and the vulnerability of the most destitute populations. The multiplicity and interdependence of objectives disqualifies cost–benefit analysis by means of a utility function as a way of getting countries to agree on the allocation of tasks for reducing the effects of climate change and adapting to them. The sole pertinent method consists in a cost–efficacy analysis that seeks to minimize the cost of securing an outcome deemed politically desirable. A criterion of fairness corresponding to considerations of 'burden sharing' must also be posited.[2]

This is what the Kyoto Protocol purported to do. It affirmed a principle of subsidiarity. Subject to an obligation to reduce their emissions, the developed countries were free to define their reduction policies for achieving their emission ceilings. The interdependence between countries participating in the accord was to be embodied in an intergovernmental international carbon market. It would produce a global price for carbon. Fairness would mark the distribution of pollution permits, which would trigger financial transfers between market participants, leading Northern countries to finance a reduction in emissions by Southern countries.

But belief in the myth of the perfect market tacked on to the Kyoto Protocol a principle of equal emission rights. Awarding emission permits does not mean granting equal emission rights to every country. The allocation of emission permits is, in effect, simply a form of allocation of financial assets. In a world with extreme inequality of wealth, the richest soon bought up the number of permits that suited them on the pollution permits market, thus circumventing this pseudo-equality. It is actual per capita emissions that must be equalized in the very long term.[3]

The Kyoto Conference was a failure because the United States refused to sign the protocol, and the principal emerging countries refused any international commitment to reduction objectives as long as the United States would not participate in an international accord. It was not until the Cancún Conference in 2010 that a change of approach emerged. The Cancún Conference of the Parties (COP 16) may be seen as a veritable fork in the road, shifting international negotiations from an insufficiently cooperative top-down game (a single carbon price based on a world market in pollution permits between states and burden-sharing), based on states' obligations, towards an international climate regime based on states' responsibility to voluntarily promote appropriate national actions that were hammered out in the Paris Accord[4] – and hence on an accumulation of bottom-up actions.

This approach, linking climate policy to development, emphasized investment in low-carbon technologies and, as a result, raised the problem of finance. In developing countries, nationally appropriate actions (NAMAs) to reduce GHG emissions lead to linking low-carbon technologies and the local environment, to investing mainly in human capacities and R&D. Here we potentially have a multiplicity of bottom-up initiatives. But the issue immediately arises of the compatibility between myriad decentralized actions and the goal of containing global climate change, once it is understood that this is the area where market failures are abiding.[5] How is the resilience of the financial system to be enhanced while redirecting a proportion of global savings to investment in low-carbon energy, means of transport, housing and urban infrastructure? NAMAs enable governments in developing countries to integrate objectives for reducing and adapting to climate change into their national development policies. This is the key condition for the participation of developing countries, including emerging countries. But GHG emissions foster a global externality. As Roger Guesnerie stresses, what is therefore required is coordination at a global level for comprehensive control of quantities. For that, countries must reach agreement on an overall emissions ceiling.

An international market in permits would regulate the gaps between the permits allocated to countries and emissions, yielding makeshift international coordination (and not on each unit of carbon emitted, as in the practical implementation of the Kyoto Protocol), while states or regional groupings of states would seek to achieve their domestic objectives with the aid of taxes and public investment policies. Compatibility between myriad decentralized actions and general climate change can in this way be ensured.

The success of the Cancún strategy involves low-carbon investment in developing countries. The World Bank sounded the alarm in 2010, indicating that financial resources were highly inadequate. This is true of the clean development mechanism, conceived in principle to generate such financing. Economic activities reducing emissions in developing countries create carbon credits that are tradeable on the European pollution permits market against unused permits held by the electricity companies. The mechanism proved completely inadequate. According to the World Bank, the finance thus obtained in 2012 for reduction and adaptation was $9 billion, whereas $17 billion per annum was needed at the start of the century, climbing to $100 billion in 2020. Income from the sale of rights decreased rapidly because of the collapse in the carbon price on the European market. Furthermore, the least advanced countries received a mere 3 per cent of the income derived from the sales! Finally, excluded from the mechanism's scope was the deforestation that is the main source of GHG emissions in tropical countries. The upshot of such woeful ineffectiveness is that developing countries are stuck with their polluting technologies.

To remedy the situation, the Green Climate Fund was created at the close of the Cancún Conference. According to the IMF, it would have to provide finance to the tune of $100 billion per annum, half for reduction and half for adaptation. For low-income countries, finance for adaptation should be provided by gifts, and finance for reduction by loans at preferential rates. The problem is that the Fund, whose headquarters is in Korea, is still not operational.

It is here that Europe – and especially France, which was due to organize the Paris Conference in December 2015 – had the opportunity to give things a decisive boost. But Europe did not propose the mechanism of monetary financing described in Chapter 9 and take charge of it. Nonetheless, in 2017 the Stiglitz–Stern commission, under the auspices of the World Bank, proposed establishing a notional carbon price, intended to create the carbon assets associated with the monetary financing of low-carbon investment projects validated by independent agencies. There is more to do in actually securing financing of the Green Climate Fund. Europe should propose that governments capitalize the Green Fund by injecting reserve assets deriving from allocations of surplus or unused special drawing rights (SDR). Shares should be determined in proportion to countries' IMF quotas. In return, contributing countries would receive capital shares in the Green Fund. On a solid capital base of $100 billion, the Fund could issue green bonds to institutional investors throughout the world, achieving leverage of up to ten, with a resulting financing capacity of $1 trillion.

In this way, the financing of climate policy would be linked to the need to advance international monetary governance by boosting the monetary role of SDR, the other area where greater symmetry is needed in a world becoming more polycentric. In both areas – climate and monetary – it will be possible to collaborate with China, which is in the process of making a major switch in anti-pollution policy, and which has already declared in favour of SDR as an ultimate reserve asset.

In Search of International Monetary Governance

If it becomes a full currency in the zone where it is supposed to be sovereign, the euro potentially has a unified government securities market of a size, depth and liquidity equivalent to that of the dollar. The euro could become the key currency in international transactions of a vast region, well beyond the eurozone proper. The problem is wholly and exclusively political. Either the eurozone advances towards a political union conferring sovereignty on the currency, or the euro will remain a secondary international currency.

In this book, I have indicated the reforms required to make the euro a full currency: banking union and fiscal union. Banking union will make it possible to unify the European financial area; fiscal union will make it possible to issue eurobonds competing with US Treasury Bonds, and thus to create the liquid market indispensable to a leading international currency.

Notwithstanding the endogenous pressures that exist for greater international stature for currencies competing with the dollar, the coexistence of currencies must still form a system. Can a multi-currency system enjoy stability? This general question prompts two further questions by way of response: What is it about the nature of money that makes competition between currencies for international monetary functions inefficient? How are we to conceive international monetary regimes as an organization of monetary relations between states achieving permanent cooperation, as opposed to circumstantial agreements that are short-lived and rapidly violated?[6]

An international monetary system is a public good in that it must be conceived, and must be capable of operating, to resolve two connected problems: on the one hand, supplying a form of liquidity accepted by all users and regulated in such a way that supply adapts to the demand created by the requirements of financing international trade; on, the other hand, making adjustments in prices and trade flows so that disequilibria in balances of payments do not accumulate and do not create vulnerabilities in the international financial system.[7]

The key currency system anchored to the dollar has failed to deliver these benefits, while proving capable of surviving and creating a latent instability, punctuated by crises. It has lasted by default in the absence of currencies competing to assume its general regulatory functions. The possibility between now and 2020 of the completion of the euro and the convertibility of the yuan could change the situation and expose the flaws in the international monetary system.

The thing about the nature of money that makes competition between currencies for international monetary functions inefficient is the uniqueness of the ultimate form of liquidity – what must be accepted by everyone and, in a national monetary area, issued by the central bank. In the international monetary arena, the key currency is an imperfect substitute in the absence of a monetary authority issuing a form of liquidity that is not the debt of any country.

It falls to the key currency to perform the role of regulating international money: orderly adjustment of balances of payments compatible with the domestic balance of countries and provision of the international liquidity demanded by expanding trade. The latter must not be excessive, lest it occasion a disorderly proliferation of capital movements, and must not be insufficient, lest it generate deflationary pressure on international prices or unduly tight constraints in the balance sheets of financial intermediaries. If the country issuing the key currency conducts its monetary policy exclusively with a view to its own interests, and is not subject in return to any constraints resulting from the disruptions its policy causes in other countries, there is no reason why issuing international currency should be compatible with the needs of other countries. This is true even with floating exchange rates, if exchange rates are determined by a dynamic of momentum – a function of perceived divergences in the macroeconomic policies pursued by the countries that matter in international trade, perceptions that do not incorporate an expectation of future equilibrium in exchange rates, because this equilibrium does not exist. The public good represented by international money is not produced.

This is what the United States has always done since the Second World War gave it commanding power in international relations.[8] The only choice it leaves to other countries is either to align with its interests, on the pretext that they are the political translation of 'universal values', or to place sufficient controls on capital movements to retain autonomy in their economic policy. The belief that hegemony is a stable model of international regulation is unrealistic as soon as one steps outside the circle of the countries that accept it. When demographic forces arise, impelling developing states to escape subjection to the dollar, this circle narrows and the ability of the key currency to play the role of substitute for an absent international currency decreases. The global public good that is international monetary stability for all countries disappears.

As we have seen in the case of the eurozone, intergovernmental coordination is sterile when it comes to managing the contradictions that flow from this asymmetry. Compromises would have to be negotiated to advance minimal international cooperation. In the heat of the financial crisis, it was possible to believe that the G20 would be the new arena in which such compromises could be concluded. As of 2010, however, the G20 lapsed into insignificance, once more pointing up the traps of ad hoc approaches in the absence of institutionalization. Negotiation is difficult to maintain, because it is only effective if it results in explicit compromises in the content of the main countries' economic policies without resort to external mediation. Faced with fluid situations, giving rise to various interpretations of each country's responsibilities, negotiation lacks general rules with which to legitimate its recommendations. It also lacks an organization to translate them into compatible courses of action in national policies, and to see that they are implemented.

To overcome these problems, institutionalized cooperation will have to establish regulatory institutions to preserve decentralized conduct in a world economy where forms of interdependence vary, with the convergence of regions previously on the margins of the international set-up.[9] As in climate negotiations, a Europe attaining political autonomy and seeking to preserve multilateralism could play a very useful mediating role in constructing international monetary governance for a multi-currency system. Its pivot is a genuinely ultimate international reserve. Today, this can only take the form of Special Drawing Rights. France, which was hostile to SDR when they were created in 1968, would distinguish itself in becoming a promoter of the extension of their use.

There are three reasons to develop SDR. The first is to correct the disadvantages of a surfeit of dollars by reducing the incentives for central banks whose currencies are not fully convertible to acquire dollars for self-insurance. The second is to allocate sufficient quantities of SDR in line with a collectively agreed rule of issue, so to avoid the fluctuations between a dollar surfeit and a dollar shortage that impact on exchange rates. If the rule of issue was counter-cyclical, it would make the IMF the embryo of an international lender of last resort. The third reason is to create a substitution account within the IMF to enable countries overloaded with dollar reserves to diversify them in an orderly fashion, without going through the exchange markets, and hence without risking provoking exchange-rate fluctuations conducive to monetary crises.[10]

For SDR to be at the heart of the international monetary system, one would have to go beyond allocation by quotas and introduce an *ex nihilo* creation in the service of a multilateral mechanism of last-resort financing. This device would put the IMF as international lender of last resort on the same footing as the central banks as national lenders of last resort. This is the only way to avoid the generalization of self-insurance – behaviour that fosters persistent disequilibria in balances of payments. Furthermore, the SDR issued from allocations by quotas, and not used by countries, could be gainfully employed to lend to countries that have unmet liquidity needs, as a tool of counter-cyclical financing.

Obviously, such monetary innovation involves a profound reform of the IMF, and this depends mainly on the governments of eurozone countries realizing that they have a common interest. To shoulder the dual task of preventing discord in macroeconomic policies and monitoring common factors of financial instability, the IMF must enlarge its political base. This entails a profound change in the distribution of powers and responsibilities among member countries. The political influence of non-Western countries must be significantly increased. Substantial revisions of shares are therefore indispensable. This reform has started with the introduction of the renminbi in the SDR basket in October 2016. The criteria adopted to define quotas and associated voting rights must completely and definitively relinquish the legacy of the bargaining power and alliances of 1944. They must be replaced by an objective formula based exclusively on economic and financial factors.

It is up to Europe to play a major role in making the IMF the instance of international monetary coordination that it has had to abandon since the end of the Bretton Woods system. Given that the multi-currency system is structured regionally, the individual representation of eurozone countries must be abolished in favour of the eurozone as a single entity. This reform will put an end to a grotesque anomaly. Currently, a group of countries that no longer possess national currencies sits separately in the general assembly of the IMF, while the second international currency has no representative to speak in its name. As a result, the Europeans have no capacity for official initiatives in the debate over how best to develop the international monetary system. There must therefore be a merger of shares and associated voting rights. This will have two advantages. First, merger will give the eurozone considerable aggregate weight. Second, merger does not mean summation. It will free up a substantial proportion of shares, which can be reassigned to the rest of the world and facilitate the intended redeployment.

This common-sense reform will have a knock-on effect on completion of the euro. It will reinforce the need for a common executive capable of promoting an aggregate economic policy, resulting in the formulation of an external monetary policy.

The other changes involve operating procedures to make the Fund more effective. It must ensure the participation of all its influential members in a multi-currency system. The Fund cannot become the central institution of international monetary governance if a halt is not called to a single country with a blocking minority usurping power within it. An amendment must reduce the qualified majority, which was fixed at 87.5 to allow the United States to exercise it single-handedly, to 75 per cent. Finally, to be able to play the key monetary role defined above, the Fund will have to take some urgent decisions. Its managing director must enjoy effective political support from a body that can be summoned rapidly, and which is of sufficient political calibre to commit the member countries. This implies promoting the Executive Board to the rank of a political council, bringing together senior officials mandated by their respective governments. This council should meet monthly, and whenever necessary in emergencies. The post of managing director itself must cease to be the preserve of the Europeans. It is high time an open selection procedure was established based exclusively on criteria of competence.

Such are the long-term developments that Europe should help foster as an extension of its own political self-assertion, and to bolster it in a multipolar world.

Afterword to the English Edition

Since this book appeared in French, some very significant political events have occurred in Europe and the United States that considerably alter the bases on which the European project has hitherto been built.

The first was the announcement of Brexit following the British referendum of June 2016. When given legal effect, the size of the European Union will be reduced, and the eurozone will account for 85 per cent of EU GDP. This will profoundly affect the logic of integration.

Fears of serious disruption in international relations raised by Trump's access to power have been confirmed by his first year at the head of the US government. Uncertainty has spread in international relations, with a major impact on Europe. From the early 1950s, the European project was based on its incorporation into an international political order under American hegemony. This arrangement avoided the issue of Europe as a political power. Consequently, Trump's rejection of the international rules involved in that hegemonic order creates geopolitical uncertainty with profound repercussions for Europe.

Finally, 2017 witnessed political upsets in the eurozone's two leading countries. In France, the two-party, left–right system broke up. The political orientation of a fluid parliamentary majority is far from clear. But the European convictions of the new president of the republic are explicit, even if his priorities as regards the opposition his proposals will arouse are not. In Germany, the simultaneous erosion of the conservative majority and the social-democratic opposition has created a governmental paralysis unknown since the creation of the Federal Republic. A compromise between the leaderships of CDU-CSU, on one side, and the SPD on the other has been painstakingly reached. It is appealing as far as a boost in European integration is concerned. But its popular approval by the rank and file of the SPD remains far from secure. If successful, the government can be set up around Easter 2018.

On the other hand, the improved economic situation has been a pleasant surprise, accompanying a general recovery in the world economy. Since mid 2016, the eurozone has experienced a rebound that seems more robust than those preceding it in 2014 and 2015, followed as they were by relapses. In fact, for the first time since 2009 the unemployment rate fell below 10 per cent in mid 2017 (9.5 per cent), thanks to projected growth of 1.8 per cent for the year. However, the scars of what has been called 'secular stagnation' are far from having disappeared.[1] The cyclical development of the eurozone remains fragile. Divergences between creditor and debtor countries persist, together with a lag in private investment, weak progress in productivity, and a weakness in public investment, which has fallen from 4 to 2 per cent of GDP since the 1980s.

The window of opportunity is possibly narrow. We must take advantage of the current bright spell to make significant progress in European integration. While progress is dependent on reform of the European budget, the issue is identifying the nature of this advance and the political reform that would take it forward.

To this end, we must first grasp the underlying reasons for the incompletion of the European project, which is being undermined by disaggregating forces. Then we must explore the idea that the European Union is more than the sum of its parts – something expressed in the potential for creating a European value added.

Incompletion of the Construction of Europe

The neo-functionalist aporia of the European project

The neo-functionalist model inspired European construction at the outset, and persists today. Applied in Jean Monnet's 'small steps' approach, neo-functionalism is regarded by its supporters as a slow, irreversible economic process of integration. It is closely associated with a horizontal conception of community law: free, undistorted competition and free circulation of mobile factors. This doctrine has been incorporated into bodies of national law under the authority of the European Court of Justice (ECJ). It fuels a dynamic that escapes the control of national governments, while hoping for an ever closer union of the peoples of Europe thanks to the efficiency gains expected from competition.

The presiding spirit of European construction in its early stages, the neo-functionalist method stopped working when it ventured into the financial sphere with the Single

European Act. The neo-functionalist approach underwent a change in kind. It became market fundamentalism – an ideology postulating efficient finance, which is self-regulating and, as a result, regulates the whole economy. In short, the apotheosis of laissez-faire.

Finance, after all, is not one economic sector among others, which can gradually be incorporated into a system of market interdependencies. Finance constructs economic time, determining the conventional procedures whereby beliefs about the future are organized. It therefore regulates the totality of economic sectors via the mediation of financial markets. The pivot of this mediation is liquidity – a highly social variable, since liquidity is demanded by everyone because everyone supposes that it is demanded by all. When the macroeconomic development of different countries is uncoordinated, finance can only exacerbate divergences between member-states, as has happened since the introduction of the euro. Divergences in debt, share and real estate prices are amplified in a logic of momentum.

As an agency of the increase in social inequalities and divergences between member-states, the financialization of the European economies revealed its noxious character by compounding the global financial crisis with a crisis of the eurozone (2012–13). In the uncoordinated responses to the crisis, state sovereignty was undermined. In the absence of European political projects to resolve the crisis, it was eroded amid a rise in populism and civic apathy. In fact, democracy cannot accommodate an unbounded horizontal economism, informed by the old ideology of 'laissez-faire'. It is nurtured by participation in the verticality of political authority: in other words, in state power.

The bedrock of modern democracy is the budget under the control of parliament. The budget alone makes it possible for voters to make a choice between major policy orientations, and hence to exercise democratic power. It follows that the European Union as an institutional entity is not a democracy. It is a machine for regulating. Only a public authority establishing a veritable European budget would be endowed with a capacity for creating, not merely regulating.

The malfunctions of European construction, exposed by the global financial crisis, stem from a collective inability to act on social reality on a continental scale by producing European public goods.

Consequently, the political issue of our time is a democratic pact at a European level, preserving the sovereignty of member-states: what might be called a dual democracy, at once national and European.[2] Its pivot is reform of the European budget. The task of a new stage in building Europe is to situate this democratic pact in the space of the political possibilities afforded by the twofold context, intra-European and global, indicated above.

The debasement of democracy in member-states

The European juridico-political order as a complex system fuels a structural dynamic atrophying the state power of member-states. It derives from a reduction in the budgetary powers of national parliaments. The EU's juridico-political order places member states in a situation of regulatory competition. In the eurozone, this increased competition, which allows only for supply-side policies, led to deflationary pressure following the financial crisis in the shape of internal devaluation, resulting in long years of recession or stagnation.

The austerity policies dictated by the inability to pursue a coordinated, Europe-wide policy in response to the eurozone crisis plunged some countries into depression. In Southern countries, households suffered a marked drop in spending power. In 2017, they had still not recovered their 2007 living standards. In Italy, per capita spending power remains 11 per cent below that of 2007. In Spain, the fall in incomes was very sharp (–12 per cent at the height of the crisis, in 2012), but the recovery wiped out some of the losses, so that 2017 living standards were 6.5 per cent below those of 2007. The position of households is much worse in Greece, where spending power fell by 30 per cent at the height of the crisis, and is now only 75 per cent of its 2007 level. By contrast, Germany made up for a lack of domestic demand by an extraordinary expansion of its external trade surplus, exceeding 9 per cent of GDP. This extraordinary surplus sustained employment sufficiently to maintain spending power growth of around 10 per cent compared with 2007. A final scenario is offered by France and the United Kingdom, where household living standards did not undergo a marked decline during the crisis, but stagnated until Spring 2016.

European fiscal rules have increasingly been subject to legislation in the eurozone, reducing the budgetary power of member-states without creating European budgetary power. In fact, the EU budget is characterized by a remarkable structural feebleness: it amounts to 1 per cent of EU GDP, the bulk of which is not the EU's own resources because it involves the contributions of member-states. As to the rule of unanimity in Council decisions, it confers an advantage on supporters of the status quo – in other words, member-states afforded a competitive advantage over others by the current set-up. The combined effect of the reduction in states' margin of action and the absence of any real budgetary capacity on the part of the EU generates a sense of public impotence, which is increasingly less acceptable to citizens.

The disconnection between single currency and national sovereignty

The creation of the euro to crown the Single European Act was unquestionably a break with the method of small steps; money is a basic institution of societies, indissolubly bound up with political sovereignty.[3] Introducing a currency in a social space where there is no single political sovereign is an innovation that was bound to pose problems. People did their best to discount them, but they fully emerged with the crisis of the eurozone from 2010.

In capitalist economies money is ambivalent, and hence at the heart of social contradictions. On the one hand, it is a collective power of society whose general acceptance affords protection to its members. On the other, it is an unlimited desire for appropriation. Liquidity is both the support and the goal of the accumulation of private wealth. The ambivalence of money derives from these contradictory aspects of the social bond. That is why the legitimate authority in charge of monetary good practice has two concerns in regulating economic time: on the one hand, maintaining the integrity of the unit of account, or monetary stability; on the other, ensuring the completion of payments, or financial stability.

Since sovereignty is exercised in the context of nations, only a legitimate power can exercise it. That is why, in nation-states, sovereignty in the monetary order is delegated by the Constitution to central banks. The European Central Bank is an exception, because it derives its legitimacy from an international treaty – the Treaty of Maastricht – whose signatories are sovereign states. The disconnection is therefore patent. In democratic states, legitimate delegation of the conduct of monetary policy is deemed to be in the service of social welfare. The central bank must maintain the monetary order as a set of civic rights and duties. For this to occur, the two orders of legitimacy – political and monetary – must be encompassed in a higher constitutional order that defines the respective powers of the two public authorities: the political executive and the central bank as guarantor of monetary integrity.

The euro is an exception, because an international treaty does not have the legitimate force of a constitutional order formalizing the collective belonging of a people. It is a weaker form of legitimacy, which severely limited the ECB's prerogatives until the crisis of the euro. In the Maastricht Treaty, relations between the ECB and the member-states were not spelled out. They were deemed unnecessary, in line with the ideology of the neutrality of money that abandoned any responsibility for financial stability, supposedly automatically achieved by the efficiency of finance. This ideology, which echoed German strategic concerns, also disavowed any involvement of monetary policy in public policy geared to growth and employment.

The crisis of the eurozone, which exploded into the open in May 2010, is not merely an aftershock of the general financial crisis that raged in 2007–08. It has internal causes in the cumulative divergences between countries since the euro was introduced. They have been facilitated by the euro's incompletion, which excluded any macroeconomic coordination in the currency zone. The European Council is an arena where national interests clash, and is at best capable of compromises dictated by circumstances, often 'on the edge of the abyss' for the most pressing subjects, but without any ability to cultivate a European interest legitimized by national democratic representations. The ECB was excluded from these compromises, since the treaty assigned it a single mission, supposedly independent of public policy. The relevant coordination was supposed to be achieved through capital markets, once 'free, undistorted competition' had been established and maintained by the ECJ.

That is why the eurozone possessed neither the common resources for action nor the clairvoyance of political leaders – still less the democratic legitimacy required to assert the long-term interests of Europe. In compelling states to come to the aid of financial sectors on the point of collapse, the devastating financial crisis created a vicious circle of deteriorating bank balance-sheets and mushrooming government debt in various member-states. The very continuity of payments in the eurozone was imperilled because the interbank market was paralyzed. This extreme situation prompted the ECB to assume the sovereign role of any central bank in the monetary sphere: lending in last resort.

These critical years demonstrated the extent to which political governance of the eurozone is ill-adapted to the character of monetary union. Indeed, in a self-maintained low-inflation regime, the separation between monetary policy and fiscal policy loses any coherence. The new fiscal treaty of March 2012 (the Treaty on Stability, Coordination and Governance, or Stability Pact) has not strengthened coordination for reaching agreement on an aggregated budgetary envelope for the eurozone, or on sharing adjustments between countries. On the contrary, it has strengthened binding rules without avoiding an increase in government debt.

Obstinate persistence with neo-functionalist logic resulted in countries being set against one another in search of competitiveness. Applied at national level, this conception – so-called internal devaluation – is nothing but a crude neomercantilism whereby every country seeks an external surplus: a game in which Germany is champion. It is perfectly clear that such a conception of the relations between countries excludes any solidarity between eurozone members in principle. Pursued within a monetary union that rules out exchange-rate adjustments, this logic generates self-destructive forces.

However, the compromise of 'solidarity in exchange for responsibility' falls into a trap at once theoretical and practical. Formulating the problem in such terms boils down to inscribing it in the logic of a zero-sum game, which inevitably leads to perpetuation of the divergences in interest between debtor states and creditor states, and hence to the creation of sub-optimal equilibria that are vulnerable to the disruption of the world economy. For significant progress in constructing Europe, what is required is a European political pact. And to envisage it, a change of doctrine is needed, which consists in accepting that the European whole is larger than the sum of its parts. The very existence of the EU creates a value added, a common surplus.[4]

I am going to explore this way of escaping the dead end of a zero-sum game that is turning into a negative-sum game in the adverse circumstances created by the global financial cycle characteristic of financialized capitalism, as has been shown by the BIS.[5] The ECB is alone in coping without any aid from member-states. I will show that only adequate policies, deploying a European budget directed by a public authority, can create a European value added by producing European public goods. These policies involve a long-term view that Europe is currently lacking.

Creating a Dual European Democracy and Transforming the Growth Regime

Proposals for overcoming the obstacles to a coherent EU, and especially the eurozone, have not been wanting recently. The French president, Emmanuel Macron, wants to make the eurozone autonomous from the European Union, by equipping it with new institutions separate from the latter: a budget, a finance minister, and a eurozone parliament with the power to raise taxes and issue debt at eurozone level independently of the EU's institutions. The German Finance Ministry is violently opposed to this suggestion, focusing its proposal on conversion of the European Stability Mechanism into a European Monetary Fund (EMF). Its mission would be to strengthen the requirement to restructure sovereign debts in exchange for the financial aid it would grant. In addition, the EMF would have the authority to compel the participation of private creditors in the restructuring process. In December 2017, the former president of the European Parliament, Martin Schulz, leader of the German SPD, adopted a position opposed to that of his country's Finance Ministry. He occasioned surprise by proposing to move towards the creation of a United States of Europe by 2025. Finally, the European Commission has presented a proposal of its own. In contrast to the Macron proposal, the Commission wants all the intergovernmental bodies of the eurozone to be integrated into the framework of the EU's institutions.

These proposals are incompatible because they are utterly opposed on the institutional order, and hence the relevant political authority, in the case of the views of Macron and the Commission. They are opposed for reasons of political tactics and ideology in the case of the two German proposals. None of them takes account of the duality of the EU's political space.

Distinguishing between sovereignty and public authority

We need to understand and accept the duality of the EU's political space. On the one hand, 'political space' refers here to the EU as a juridico-political entity created by the treaties signed and ratified by member-states. This entity is autonomous, because it possesses its own juridico-political order. On the other hand, it refers to the entity formed by the merging of member-states, each of them deploying its own sovereign juridico-political order. This constitutive duality contains, and often confounds, two distinct juridico-political levels, which are autonomous but nevertheless closely linked: namely, the EU in the strict sense and the entity formed by the association of member-states. That is why a federal leap, encompassing the two levels in an overarching sovereignty, is impossible as long as it is not desired and accepted by the citizens of Europe. In fact, this would involve a leap in sovereignty, which would require a constituent act. Indeed, sovereignty is indissolubly one and indivisible in a given political space. Full, integral federal sovereignty is a dead end that is the mirror of the neo-functionalist dead end, converted into the market fundamentalism which aims to dissolve national sovereignty into the horizontality of market rules.

To advance on the path of integration, we have to affirm that it is member-states that are sovereign. They are the masters of the treaties, and have the right and power to leave the EU. It is therefore necessary to conceive of an EU that is democratic because it would be endowed with public authority, but without sovereignty. Democracy is not equivalent to sovereignty. Sovereign political entities exist that are not democracies. And political spaces with democratic institutions exist that are not sovereign.

The necessity of reforming the European budget

Making democracy our starting-point enables us to anchor ourselves in the paradigm of the collective capacity to make and do – the paradigm of public power. The crisis of Europe is a crisis of the capacity to supply citizens with answers to their concerns, at EU and member-state levels alike. It is an inability to implement public policies that change the course of existence. This power can be established at EU level by a

European budget orientated and controlled by the European Parliament. Such is the qualitative change of our time, comparable to those of the Treaty of Rome in 1957 and the Maastricht Treaty in 1992.

Conceived as a dual democracy, the European political system brings into play both the democratic level of the EU, which demands an EU public authority with its own budgetary capacity, enabling the emergence of a genuinely democratic life at EU level; and the democratic level of member-states, which must recover their budgetary capacity in order to restore democratic substance to national political life. And the fact that the EU is equipped with budgetary capacity will make it possible to 'return' budgetary power to member-states, particularly their parliaments, and hence make possible fiscal coordination that is effective because it is legitimate and politically accepted by citizens.

Two temporal dimensions must be distinguished, allocating the roles of public authority at EU and national levels. The EU must play a pioneering role in the advent of a regime of sustainable growth, based on a new social contract. This prospect indicates the need for a European public authority based on deployment of the European budget, renewed in the search for a European value added created by long-term investment. In the time of the economic cycle, the eurozone must effect more symmetrical adjustments between countries in the framework of a counter-cyclical policy for the whole eurozone. This implies reform of the procedure of the European Semester to introduce a mechanism conducive to more symmetrical macroeconomic adjustments.

The European budget: European value added and 'own resources'

The long-term dimension is crucial for initiating a new stage in European integration. It is indispensable for promoting sustainable development that involves investment in public infrastructure and in the environment and human resources, which exceeds the capacities of individual states. Europe represents the appropriate scale for investment that produces a European value added. In accordance with the principle of dual democracy, it will be for citizens during European elections to choose European policy priorities.

European value added is generated by European public policies with an impact over and above the value that could be created by each country separately, in line with the principle of subsidiarity. It is therefore necessary to identify investments linked to policy objectives yielding overall gains, not merely local ones. Collective benefit is a common good. The outcome includes synergies due to externalities (reduction in future damage from climate change through low-carbon investment now); transnational network effects (energy interconnections, digital and transport networks); and policies of regional cohesion that must be greatly expanded to multiply forms of transnational cooperation (education, training, health and social inclusion). European value added is the economic advantage that helps create a shared awareness of European affiliation in national civil societies.

In contemporary financial capitalism, such long-range investment comes up against the tragedy of the horizon: it must confront systemic risks liable to manifest themselves far beyond the horizons of the economic and political decision-makers currently in office.

This is especially the case with systemic climatic risk and its impact on finance. It derives from radical uncertainty about the climate's impact on economies. This kind of uncertainty means changing the relations between finance and politics, as it requires collective insurance mechanisms very far removed from what exists in today's financial globalization. More fundamentally, an ethical principle of social justice is indispensable to the democratic acceptability of imposing inter-temporal choices at European level. Yet the electoral cycles of present-day national democratic regimes do not ensure continuity in European political orientation. That is why a fully fledged European budget, under the control of a European Parliament detached from national partisan jousting, would be a decisive step towards overcoming the tragedy of the horizon, with a view to a European value added.

In the current situation, the European budget is a zero-sum game. National governments are interested only in the sum total of their contributions to the European budget and what they get in return. It must be transformed into a 'win–win' budget by allocating it to programmes that yield a European value added. For the budget to be able to help finance, but above all guarantee, investment intended to generate European value added, its size must be increased and its own resources enhanced. European bodies have recently presented contributions to this end: the Monti group's report on the future financing of Europe and the European Commission's contribution on the future of EU finances.

Increasing the European budget's own resources must make it possible to pursue policies geared to long-term investment. Own resources are resources definitively vested in the Union's budget. They are tax revenues allocated to Europe for the purpose of pursuing common policies. They are not expenditures from national budgets transferred to Europe, but subject to national budgetary decisions. Currently, only the bulk of customs duties (80 per cent) pertain to the European budget independently of decisions by member-states.

To expand the budget, the political connection must be made between own resources, democratic legitimacy and European value added. This link would impart indirect fiscal power to the European Parliament on the basis of democratic decisions by national parliaments about sharing Europe's total fiscal resources. An increase in own resources would expand the field of European policies. New own resources can be justified by long-term investment policies that strengthen European integration, creating European value added: a tax on CO_2, a tax on electricity consumption warranted by the integration of distribution networks, and a tax on financial transactions warranted by unified capital markets.

Producing European public goods

To revive the democratic imperative in Europe, the growth regime must be transformed throughout Europe. The two dimensions of renewal are long-term investment to produce European value added and a reduction in divergences in the macroeconomic stabilization of the eurozone.

An EU investment policy must endeavour to reduce the enormous disparities both between member-states and between regions in individual countries. For long-term investment, let us recall, institutional reform consists in a European budget with enough of its own resources to be principally a budget of guarantees for financing common goods with European value added, guided by the recommendations of the European Parliament and provided for by an ability to issue eurobonds. Macroeconomic stabilization of the eurozone must pursue the dual objective of a counter-cyclical mechanism and a reduction in the polarization between member-states. The two dimensions are not independent if the investment strategy increases long-term growth in Europe.

Long-term investment, in pursuit of sustainable and inclusive growth, involves two priorities. One is establishing European leadership in the area of climate transition and the connected spheres of urban renewal, low-carbon infrastructure, the transformation of agriculture in the direction of soil rehabilitation, the reconstruction of ecosystems, and improved food provision as against standardized productivity agriculture. The other is developing social investment on the basis of a pact attached to the European Strategic Investment Fund (ESIF). We must reverse the destructive tendency of the 'brain drain', which causes agglomeration and polarization effects between the centres and peripheries of megacities and is destructive of inclusive growth. Any mass migration should be covered by compensating the countries or regions of departure in the form of capital or debt reduction.

Finance for long-term investment

To say that the priority of the European budget must be guaranteeing investment in disadvantaged countries that generates greater European value added is to say that it is necessary to encourage financial actors capable of financing the long term by overcoming the tragedy of horizons – for example, short-termism under the obsession of liquidity, which paralyzes market finance. Europe has an opportunity to secure public development banks and public investors. It is absurd that these actors do not participate more actively in the Juncker plan as ESIF shareholders. It is possible to increase the Fund's financial resources significantly by creating a network of all long-term public investors under the coordination of the European Investment Bank. The second category of actors to be called upon is responsible institutional investors – those who take account of ESG (environmental, social and governance) criteria when allocating the savings entrusted to them. The third category of financial actors with social responsibility is the European system of central banks. In a world of persistently low inflation, the dogma of the long-term neutrality of money, which claims to justify the absence of any relationship between budget and money, is meaningless – as is the independence of money from finance, which excludes the central bank from its responsibility for financial stability. Central banks are concerned with the financial impact of long-term fiscal policy.

*Making macroeconomic stabilization
of the eurozone more effective and fairer*

Macroeconomic stabilization of the eurozone requires a reform of the European Semester. This budgetary procedure involves each country separately. It takes no account of the macroeconomic interdependence between eurozone members, and hence of the enormous divergence in their balance of payments. This has resulted in excessive budgetary constraints on deficit countries, which have plunged them into recession. It presupposes that countries must have primary surpluses, that much larger when the repayment costs of inherited debts are high. This requirement destroys public services in those countries. That is why the ECB acts to limit the costs of servicing these debts so far as it can. Finally, and above all, the present procedure does not impose any constraints on countries in external surplus, whatever its size.

The European Semester has to be reformed in two key respects. On the one hand, fiscal policies must be coordinated so that the eurozone as a whole pursues a countercyclical policy, even if it does not possess a budget specifically for stabilization. On the other hand, relative adjustments must not be placed under the false constraint of price competitiveness, which is not conducive to managing the interdependence of countries in a monetary union.

Taking account of the macroeconomic dimension of the eurozone's situation in order to define the aggregate budgetary orientation, compatible with the perceived macroeconomic cycle in the next budget round, is the role of a putative European budgetary agency. Its role would be to identify alternative scenarios for the eurozone's prospective macro-economic situation in the world economy, given the anticipated contingencies. On this basis, it can propose counter-cyclical policies in the form of aggregate amounts of budgetary expenditures and balances appropriate for each scenario. This technical agency should comprise experts from the European Commission and national public finance offices. It could be chaired by the chair of the Eurogroup, assisted by the vice-president of the Commission responsible for macroeconomic affairs. For this procedure to acquire the democratic legitimacy at present completely wanting in the European Semester, it should be confirmed by the European Parliament sitting as a eurozone body.

The mechanism for adjustment between countries must avoid construing the social exclusively as a cost, on the pretext of competitiveness. It must take into account the aggregate level of fiscal adjustment resulting from the approach above, and emerge from a debate involving national parliaments that takes account of member-states' macroeconomic circumstances – in particular the balance of payments – so as to avoid excessive surpluses. This approach can and must reduce asymmetrical adjustments. Thus, the eurozone and member-state levels would interact in a procedure that is effective and fair.

Rediscovering the historical meaning of the European project

In its critical moments, history requires a founding political act to get out of a rut. The creation of the Common Market was one, and the establishment of the single currency another. Today, it means fighting for the creation of a European political budget. This could anchor a developing European democracy so that the totality of the European Union and its member-states achieves the status of global power, rendered indispensable by the collapse of the post-war world order.

Paris, December 2017

Notes

Introduction

1 Michel Aglietta, *Zone euro: éclatement ou fédération* (Paris: Michalon, 2011).

1 What Form Has Economic Policy Taken since the Greek Crisis?

1 See Thomas Grjebine, 'D'une crise à l'autre: 30 ans de globalisation des cycles immobiliers', *La Lettre du CEPII* 342 (March 2014).

2 Demonstration of the financial cycle and its consequences for the instability of globalized finance is largely derived from research work by the Bank for International Settlements (BIS). For a summary, see Claudio Borio, 'The Financial Cycle and Macroeconomics: What Have We Learnt?', *BIS Working Papers* 395 (December 2012).

3 These securities comprised pools of credit in housing that had become insolvent; they were coupled with mortgages on property assets whose prices had collapsed.

4 This is the rate of unemployment compatible with the optimal employment that can be achieved and maintained by means of macroeconomic policies. To improve on it, education, professional training and re-training policies are required – in short, a highly active policy for lifetime employment.

5   The concept of a natural interest rate was developed by the Swedish economist Knut Wicksell, whose ideas influenced both Keynes on monetary theory and Schumpeter on the economic cycle. The fundamental work expounding the theory is Wicksell's *Interest and Prices* (London: Macmillan, 1898).

6   The market rate cannot fall below zero, because it is always possible to convert liquid securities whose remuneration is tending to become negative into central bank notes whose nominal remuneration is zero, without restrictions or time limits. On the other hand, it is possible – and the ECB does it – to impose negative rates on bank deposits at the central bank, so as to compel banks to use these deposits. This is not a monetary policy, but an implicit tax.

7   In effect, the natural interest rate is the net marginal rate of return on capital adjusted for risk. The market rate is the base cost of loans, adjusted for risk and term. If the natural rate is higher than the market rate, opportunities exist in the economy for borrowing in order to spend. Aggregate demand can increase and production expand. A multiplier effect is triggered through a rise in incomes and expenditure until the point at which the market rate reaches the level of the natural rate.

8   On fiscal multipliers, especially their high level in a situation of economic stagnation, entailing that the pursuit of fiscal consolidation in such a context must be slow and cautious, see Michel Aglietta and Thomas Brand, *Un New Deal pour l'Europe* (Paris: Odile Jacob, 2013), pp. 155–61.

9   Secular stagnation is an old idea advanced to explain the great difficulty experienced by Western economies in recovering from the Great Depression. The author who formulated it most clearly was Alvin Hansen, in a 1939 article entitled 'Economic Progress and Declining Population Growth' (*American Economic Review* 29: 1, pp. 1–15). The idea made a strong comeback during the IMF economic forum in November 2013,

and was popularized in an article by Lawrence Summers published in the *Financial Times* (15 December 2013) entitled 'Why Stagnation Might Prove to Be the New Normal'. The World Bank seized on it next: see Otaviano Canuto, Raj Nallari and Breda Griffith, 'Sluggish Growth: Policies, Stagnation and Outlook', *Economic Premise*, World Bank, no. 139 (April 2014). Anglo-American reflections on the subject have been collected in a book edited by Coen Teulings and Richard Baldwin, *Secular Stagnation: Facts, Causes and Cures* (London: CEPR, 2014).

2 What Institutional Initiatives Have Been Taken since the Crisis?

1 The theory of the currency as social bond and the forms of trust that flow from it are set out in Michel Aglietta and André Orléan, eds, *La Monnaie souveraine* (Paris: Odile Jacob, 1998).

2 The ambivalence of the currency is the crucial concept that makes it possible to understand both the diversity of monetary systems, arranging rules through which the currency is organized to overcome the contradictions that derive from these two aspects of the currency, and monetary crises, which are episodes in which contradictions submerge the established rules and lead to the need to re-found the monetary order. On this, see Michel Aglietta and André Orléan, *La Monnaie entre violence et confiance* (Paris: Odile Jacob, 2002).

3 A rule proposed by Henri Sterdyniak in 'Ramener à zero le deficit public doit-il être l'objectif central de la politique économique?', *Les Notes de l'OFCE* 17 (April 2012).

3 Which Handicaps Have Been Exacerbated in the Eurozone?

1 See Michel Aglietta and Xavier Ragot, 'Érosion du tissu productif en France: causes et remèdes', *France Stratégie*, December 2014.

2 Paul Krugman, theoretician of the new geographical economics, has shown that the dynamic of increasing returns leads to industrial polarization, and warned Europe's leaders of this as early as 1992. See Paul Krugman, 'EMU and the Regions (Occasional Paper 39)', Group of Thirty, 1992.

3 Recently, the director of Berlin's DIW (a powerful social science institute), Marcel Fratzscher, shook his compatriots in an as yet untranslated book, whose unequivocal title is *The Illusion of Germany*.

4 Does France Have a Particular Impairment?

1 Jean-Marc Pillu and Yves Zlotowski, 'PME françaises: fragiles et indispensables', *Revues d'économie financière* 114 (2014).

2 Jean-Louis Beffa, *La France doit choisir* (Paris: Seuil, 2012).

3 See Michel Aglietta and André Réberioux, *Dérives du capitalisme financier* (Paris: Albin Michel, 2004), Chapter 2, 'Critique des fondements de la valeur actionnariale'.

4 Olivier Passet, 'La France dans dix ans: quelle évolution de notre modèle productif?', *Xerfi Synthèse* 3 (November 2013).

5 Laurent Faibis and Olivier Passet, 'Politique publique et transition économique', Conference on the Economic Transition: A New Wave of Growth, 14 March 2014.

6 Olivier Passet, 'Politique de baisse des charges: attention aux fausses certitudes sur le déficit français en emplois peu qualifiés', *Xerfi Synthèse* 6 (May 2014).

7 Dorothée Kohler and Jean-Daniel Weisz, *Pour un nouveau regard sur le Mittelstand*, La Documentation française, October 2012.

8   See the report directed by Jean-Pierre Aubert, 'Mutations socio-économiques et territoires: les ressources de l'anticipation', September 2014.

5   How Should European Finance be Reorganized?

1   This is defined more completely in the Afterword, below.
2   BIS Annual Report, 29 June 2014, Chapter 6, 'The Financial System at a Crossroads', at bis.org.
3   Adrien Béranger, Jézabel Couppey-Soubeyrand and Laurence Scialom, 'Union bancaire: le temps joue contre nous', *Terra Nova*, May 2014.
4   BIS Annual Report, 29 June 2014, p. 112.
5   Anat Admati and Martin Hellwig, *The Bankers' New Clothes: What's Wrong with Banking and What to Do about It* (Princeton: Princeton University Press, 2013).
6   This key result of 'orthodox' financial theory is known as the Modigliani-Miller theorem. It is completely opposed to Keynes's theory, which is based on radical uncertainty (see the following section).
7   Tobias Adrian, Daniel Covitz and Nellie Liang, 'Financial Stability Monitoring', *Fed NY Staff Reports* 601 (February 2013).
8   See Chapter 6 for a detailed discussion.
9   With a few exceptions, these two regulatory forms cover Continental Europe and the Anglo-American countries (OECD, 2010).
10   The study forms Chapter 3 of *World Economic Outlook*, October 2014, and is entitled 'Is It Time for an Infrastructure Push? The Macroeconomic Effects of Public Investment', at imf.org.
11   Natacha Valla, Thomas Brand and Sébastien Doisy, 'A New Architecture for Public Investment in Europe', *CEPII Policy Brief* 4 (July 2014).

6 How Can Public Finances be Made Sustainable without Stifling the Economy?

1   Carmen Reinhart and Kenneth Rogoff, *Growth in Time of Debt*, NBER Working Paper no. 15639 (January 2010) – a text that triggered an impassioned debate over the negative impact on growth of a debt exceeding 90 per cent of GDP. This econometric study, on the basis of evidence from a number of countries, concluded that, above 90 per cent, a rise in government debt had a negative impact on growth. Seeking to repeat the result, three economists – Thomas Herndon, Michael Ash and Robert Pollin – found, on the contrary, a positive relationship: above 90 per cent, as below 90 cent, an increase in government debt boosts GDP, even if the multiplier is weaker than in the debt tiers of 30–60 per cent and 60–90 per cent. The reason for the difference was a coding error by Reinhart and Rogoff, which led to a truncated sample and calculation errors. See Thomas Herndon, Michael Ash and Robert Pollin, *Does Public Debt Consistently Stifle Growth? A Critique of Reinhart and Rogoff*, Political Economy Research Institute Working Paper no. 322 (April 2013).

2   Andrea Pescatori, Damiano Sandri and John Simon, *Debt and Growth: Is There a Magic Threshold?*, IMF Working Paper, February 2014.

3   The first report is Michel Aglietta et al., *Finances publiques: l'épreuve de vérité pour la zone euro*, September 2011; and the second is Michel Aglietta et al., *Dettes publiques en zone euro: enseignements de l'histoire et stratégie pour l'avenir*, July 2014. These inquiries were carried out with the support of the Institut CDC pour la Recherche and were published by Groupe Caisses des Dépôts.

4   Hansjörg Blöchliger, Dae-Ho Song and Douglas Sutherland, *Fiscal Consolidation Part 4: Case Studies of Large Fiscal*

Consolidation Episodes, OECD Economics Department Working Papers no. 935, OECD Publishing, 2012.

5   The dollar fell enormously in 1985–87 against all other convertible currencies. In September 1987, the Fed tried to halt its decline by raising its interest rate. This led to a violent stock market panic in October, following which the Fed executed a hasty policy U-turn, restarting the dollar's depreciation against the yen. Going into debt in dollars and lending in yen to finance property speculation afforded Japanese banks, which were not concerned about the risk of exchange-rate fluctuations, a comfortable margin that encouraged them to support the speculative wave without putting a limit on corporate leverage. The bursting of the speculative bubble in 1990 caused a fall in the yen, and was a disaster for the banks, which were hit simultaneously by the insolvency of their loans and by exchange-rate losses.

6   A full study by Gilles Gufrénot and Karim Triki can be found in Aglietta et al., *Dettes publiques en zone euro*, Chapter 3.

7   See Aglietta et al., *Dettes publiques en zone euro*, pp. 102–7.

7   How Can Fiscal Union Be Advanced?

1   Robert E. Wright, *One Nation under Debt: Hamilton, Jefferson and the History of What We Owe* (New York: McGraw-Hill, 2008).

2   The now classic book setting out the economic functions of the state that determine the structure of public finances is Richard Musgrave, *The Theory of Public Finance* (New York: McGraw-Hill, 1959).

3   Optimum currency areas are something of a hotchpotch: lists of economic criteria, unrelated to one another, exist, whose authors decree that an optimum currency area exists, and hence that currencies can be unified without any danger of the unified currency being incomplete. Three celebrated contributions on the subject are Robert

A. Mundell, 'A Theory of Optimum Currency Areas', *American Economic Review* 51: 4 (1961); Ronald I. McKinnon, 'Optimum Currency Areas', *American Economic Review* 53: 4 (1963); and Peter Kenen, 'The Theory of Optimum Currency Areas: An Eclectic View', *Monetary Problems of the International Economy* (Chicago: University of Chicago Press, 1969).

4   *Les Notes du CAE* 3 (April 2013), at cae-eco.fr.

5   Henrik Enderlein, Lucas Guttenberg and Jan Spiess, *Une assurance contre les chocs conjoncturels dans la zone euro*, Études & Rapports 100, Jacques Delors Institute (September 2013).

6   See Jürgen Habermas, *The Crisis of the European Union: A Response*, transl. Ciaran Cronin (Cambridge: Polity, 2012).

7   Sylvie Goulard and Mario Monti, *De la démocratie en Europe* (Paris: Flammarion, 2012).

8   Can a New Social Contract be Established?

1   Pierre Rosanvallon, *La Société des égaux* (Paris: Éditions du Seuil, 2011).

2   Michel Aglietta, *A Theory of Capitalist Regulation: The US Experience*, transl. David Fernbach (London/New York: Verso, 2015 [1979]).

3   Assessment of the key issues in collective human resources is the subject of research undertaken by the circle of European Human Resources Directors (HRD) Circle. For an appraisal of this work, see Yves Barou, ed., *Patrimoine humain de l'entreprise et compétitivité* (Paris: Les Îlots de résistance, 2014).

4   See Michel Aglietta and Antoine Rébérioux, 'Financialization and the Firm', Chapter 23 in Michael Dietricht and Jackie Krafft, eds, *Handbook on the Economics and Theory of the Firm* (Cheltenham: Edward Elgar, 2012).

5   Guillaume Duval, *L'entreprise efficace à l'heure de Swatch et McDonald's* (Paris: Syros, 1998), pp. 165–76.

6   See the comprehensive work published by the OECD, *Inégalités hommes-femmes. Il est temps d'agir*, OECD, 2012.

7   Kenneth Arrow, *Social Choices and Individual Values*, 2nd edn (New York: Wiley, 1963).

8   John Rawls, *A Theory of Justice* (New York: Oxford University Press, 1971).

9   Amartya Sen, *The Idea of Justice* (London: Penguin, 2010).

9   What Form Would a Sustainable Growth Regime Compatible with the Ecological Transition Take?

1   The United Nations is piloting programmes on the human dimensions of development and the environment that periodically combine forces to produce a report on inclusive, sustainable wealth that goes beyond the conventions of the official system of national accounting to arrive at an exhaustive measure of the wealth of nations. The most complete available report is UNU-IHDP and UNEP, *Inclusive Wealth Report 2012: Measuring Progress towards Sustainability* (Cambridge: Cambridge University Press, 2012).

2   Joseph Stiglitz, Amartya K. Sen and Jean-Pierre Fitoussi, *Mismeasuring Our Lives: Why GDP Doesn't Add Up* (New York: New Press, 2010).

3   Michel Aglietta, 'Sustainable Growth: Do We Really Measure the Challenge?', in *Measure for Measure: Do We Measure Development?*, proceedings of the AFD-EUDN conference, 2010, AFD, December 2011.

4   See the detailed study by the Terra Nova think tank: Marine Girardé, Pierre Musseau and Christophe Schramm, *La Transition énergétique allemande*, Terra Nova, June 2014.

5   'Institutional Investors and Green Infrastructure Investments', OECD Report, October 2013.

6 Jean-Charles Hourcade, P. R. Shukla and Christophe Cassen, 'Climate Policy Architecture for the Cancun Paradigm Shift: Building upon the Lessons of History', *International Environmental Agreement*, Special Issue, 2014.

7 Michel Aglietta et al., 'Financing Transition in an Adverse Context: Climate Finance beyond Carbon Finance', *International Environmental Agreement*, Special Issue, 2014.

8 Vincent Aurez and Jean-Claude Lévy, *Économie circulaire, écologie et reconstruction industrielle?* (Paris: CDNC, 2013).

9 See the report led by Jean-Pierre Aubert, *Mutations socio-économiques et territoires: les ressources de l'anticipation*, Conseil de Développement, Brest, September 2014.

10   What Is Europe's Role in the New Era of Globalization?

1 This is the position adopted by Dani Rodrik following an analysis that aims to demonstrate the inability of a market system to regulate the relations between rival economic powers. See Dani Rodrik, *The Globalization Paradox* (New York: Norton, 2011).

2 Nicholas Stern stresses the need for an ethical principle to guide climate negotiations. See Roger Guesnerie and Nicholas Stern, *Deux économistes face au changement climatique* (Paris: Le Pommier, 2012), pp. 93–7.

3 As Nicholas Stern clearly puts it, if the world must emit fewer than 20 billion tons of CO_2 equivalents in 2050, it will be necessary, given that the planet will have around 9 billion inhabitants, to limit emissions everywhere to 2 tons of CO_2 equivalent per capita in 2050.

4 Nationally Appropriate Mitigation Actions for developing countries and Nationally Determined Contributions for all countries.

5   Guesnerie and Stern, *Deux économistes face au changement climatique.*

6   These questions have been addressed in detail in Michel Aglietta and Virginie Coudert, *Le Dollar et le système monétaire international* (Paris: La Découverte, 2014). The arguments that follow are based on the analyses and proposals offered there.

7   See ibid., Chapter 4.

8   Barry Eichengreen, *Exorbitant Privilege* (Oxford: Oxford University Press, 2011).

9   It involves establishing an international monetary regime that supervises countries' economic policies in accordance with common principles, rules of action that avert destabilizing discord between national policies, and procedures of coordination and common surveillance under the auspices of the IMF. For a theoretical definition of international regimes, see Robert Keohane, *After Hegemony* (Princeton: Princeton University Press, 1984).

10 When the substitution account was seriously envisaged in 1979, Jacques Polak, adviser to the IMF's managing director, argued for SDR to be put at the heart of the IMF. See his 'Thoughts on an IMF Based Fully on SDR', International Monetary Fund, Pamphlet Series 28 (1979). See also Peter Kenen, 'Reforming the Global Reserve Regime: The Role of the Substitution Account', *International Finance* 13: 1 (2010).

Afterword to the English language edition

1   Secular stagnation is defined as an economy's persistent inability simultaneously to achieve full employment, an inflation target and financial stability.

2   See Michel Aglietta and Nicolas Leron, *La double démocratie* (Paris: Éditions du Seuil, 2017).

3   Compare Michel Aglietta, *Money: 5,000 Years of Debt and Power*, transl. David Broder, (London/New York: Verso, 2018).

4   It is worth noting that the Monti report refers to 'European value added'. Compare the report of the High Level Group on Own Resources for the EU, January 2017.

5   See Claudio Borio, 'The Financial Cycle and Macroeconomics: What Have We Learnt?', *Journal of Banking and Finance* 45 (August 2014).